Love Heals

"*Love Heals* is a captivating book leading you into healing your whole person. As you will discover early on, Sonja Corbitt writes beautifully and with deep insight into the human heart. She is a trusted guide, having been on this journey herself while leading many others into the depths of their souls to discover God's transforming love in the midst of their brokenness. Whether you are just beginning or have been on a healing journey for a while, you will love this book."

Bob Schuchts
Author of *Be Healed*

"For many years, Sonja Corbitt has written books that have been of great benefit to her readers, including me! And this book, *Love Heals*, is no exception. In it, Corbitt gently shines a light on many hidden things in our hearts, bringing much-needed teaching and counsel about being healed and transformed by love. Her passion and desire for believers to be whole are evident on every page, and she leads us in a relaxed, personal, and easy-to-read style. This is a timely book that you will want to read and share."

Barbara Heil
Founder of From His Heart Ministries

"I am praising God for the way Sonja Corbitt so beautifully and passionately extends the healing work of Jesus Christ in the world today. Her personal stories are achingly rich, her scriptural illustrations are riveting, and her teaching is, as usual, brilliantly eye-opening. *Love Heals* goes on my 'game-changer' shelf."

Claire Dwyer
Author of *This Present Paradise* and cofounder of Write These Words

"Healing is never merely psychological, physical, emotional, or spiritual. For the person longing for a more integrated approach to healing that is aligned with God's plan of salvation for their lives, *Love Heals* gives the practical lessons and steps to reframe healing and suffering as a journey into deeper love with the Lord. After reading, you may even start to welcome suffering as a gift!"

Matt Ingold
Cofounder of Metanoia Catholic

Love Heals

A Biblical Plan to Restore Our Emotions, Memories, Souls, and Bodies

A Study of the Great Commandment

Sonja Corbitt

Ave Maria Press AVE Notre Dame, Indiana

Unless otherwise specified, scripture quotations are from *Revised Standard Version: Catholic Edition*, copyright © 1965, 1966 the Division of Christian Education of the National Council of the Churches of Christ in the United States of America. Used by permission. All rights reserved worldwide.

Passages marked *CCC* are from the English translation of the *Catechism of the Catholic Church* for the United States of America copyright © 1994, United States Catholic Conference, Inc.—Libreria Editrice Vaticana. Used with Permission. Published with ecclesiastical approval.

LOVE the Word® and the STOP Tool™ are trademarked to the author, Sonja Corbitt.

Nihil Obstat: Reverend Justin N. Raines, STL
　　　　　　　Censor Librorum
Imprimatur: Very Reverend John J. H. Hammond, JCL
　　　　　　　Vicar General, Diocese of Nashville
　　　　　　　Given at Nashville, Tennessee, on 22 October 2024

The *Nihil Obstat* and *Imprimatur* are official declarations that a book or pamphlet is free of doctrinal or moral error. No implication is contained therein that those who have granted the *Nihil Obstat* or *Imprimatur* agree with its contents, opinions, or statements expressed.

© 2025 by Sonja Corbitt

All rights reserved. No part of this book may be used or reproduced in any manner whatsoever, except in the case of reprints in the context of reviews, without written permission from Ave Maria Press®, Inc., P.O. Box 428, Notre Dame, IN 46556, 1-800-282-1865.

Founded in 1865, Ave Maria Press is a ministry of the United States Province of Holy Cross.

www.avemariapress.com

Paperback: ISBN-13 978-1-64680-373-6

E-book: ISBN-13 978-1-64680-374-3

Cover image © Getty Images.

Cover and text design by Brianna Dombo.

Printed and bound in the United States of America.

Library of Congress Cataloging-in-Publication Data is available.

Contents

Introduction: Healed for Love, by Love **vii**

1. *Healing Is Sacred*
   The Great Commandment as Our Template for Wholeness **1**

2. *With All Your Heart*
   Jesus Heals the Blind . . . and Teaches Us to See **11**

3. *With All Your Soul*
   Jesus Revives the Woman at the Well . . . Why Judgments Can Help You Heal **39**

4. *With All Your Mind*
   Jesus Heals Deafness . . . and Transforms Toxic Thinking **71**

5. *With All Your Strength*
   Jesus Restores the Paralytic . . . and Heals Our Bodies **91**

6. *The Sum of Your Loves*
   Tools for Continued Whollyness **127**

Notes **138**

Introduction

Healed for Love, By Love

You've heard all your life that the first and greatest commandment is to love the Lord your God with all your heart, soul, mind, and strength (see Mark 12:30). But what does that even mean—and where do we begin?

The first step is understanding that God commands that we love him, not for his benefit, but for ours: the first and greatest commandment is a template for whole-person healing. God's love has the power to heal every part of us: painful emotions, fears, and memories; unforgiveness, judgments, deficits, and wounds of love; oppressive, anxious, negative thoughts; and weary, diseased bodies.

We are commanded to love God, first, because love heals. We are healed by Love, for love.

If you've never experienced healing, but have areas in your life that need it; if you've been to a healing retreat or Mass and received a miraculous healing, only for the suffering to return later; if you've prayed and prayed for healing and been met by heaven's roaring silence; if you've experienced relief in a wound or sin habit through deliverance, only for it to be reactivated sometime afterward; if you've become frustrated or confused by the slowness or seeming impermanence of your emotional or physical healing: this book will show you why and give you tools to navigate the bewilderment and move forward in sustained healing.

You're in good company. After all, every person Jesus healed in the Bible was sent back into his life in the same ways. Even

Lazarus—who was resurrected—lived and suffered to die again afterward. Why?

Because there's always *more* love to receive and give; in his stunning generosity, God is growing our capacity for love, thereby growing the capacity for love in the whole world.

The word *salvation* in the Bible is a big, full word meaning wholeness, integration, peace, and healing. Healing is the whole point of salvation, as Pope Benedict XVI observed: "Healing is an essential dimension of the apostolic mission and of Christian faith in general. When understood at a sufficiently deep level, this expresses the entire content of redemption."[1]

Love saves us. We are healed by love; we are healed for love. Healing is your rightful inheritance as a child of God through Jesus Christ. We must learn how to receive and give *authentic* love—from the heart, soul, mind, and strength—the first and greatest commandment. Jesus knows that this is the way into a Reality so deep, so profound, and so transformative that you will finally understand why the Gospel is "Good News" if you allow the message to penetrate. He invites you to open your emotional, intellectual, spiritual, and physical wounds to him so he can pour his love into them, so you can pour that love into your neighbor.

So, how do you receive this healing? How do you begin to heal?

The "science of love," as St. Thérèse of Lisieux frames it, follows the first and greatest commandment, involving . . .

your heart's *emotions*,
your soul's *judgments*,
your mind's *thoughts*, and
your body's symptoms.

The poetic language of the Bible—which separates heart, soul, mind, and strength in the Great Commandment—should not be interpreted too literally. The Bible is not a psychological or anthropological document; it is God's revelation of himself to us that reveals the story of our salvation. The human person is a composite of body and soul so that isolating one part of the person from the rest is somewhat imprecise from a Catholic anthropological point of view, even while doing so fits beautifully within the spiritual sense of scripture.

For example, St. Thomas Aquinas specified that emotion is meant to be governed by the rational spirit in order to move us to proper action, so it involves the heart, soul, mind, and strength. In the sense that emotions are the language of the heart and speak accurately about wounds of the heart—as in having a "broken heart"—we can address the heart's emotions and memories. I treat the soul's judgments, the mind's lies, and the body's symptoms similarly.

Therefore, this is the outline of the content for this book, which is both an introductory summary of the comprehensive Love Heals Masterclass offered through my ministry and based on it. I have led innumerable Christians—through both my public ministry and one-on-one—to deeper, more permanent healing through the Holy Spirit's use of the tools in this book.

Love flows to us from the Holy Trinity through the *uncreated* Immaculate Heart of the Holy Spirit and his spouse, Mary, the *created* Immaculate Heart, taught St. Maximilian Kolbe.[2] So, we begin where the Trinity begins: with his Word, with love, and with the heart, the reservoir of love.

You'll learn how Jesus heals blindness, an inability to see the pattern and wound at the heart of your suffering, and how to cooperate with the Holy Spirit who is working there to heal your heart wounds and their corresponding emotions and memories. Why do you keep being hurt in the same ways?

Since peace is a gift from God, you'll learn how to stop spiritual harassment. Toxic "forgiveness" is torment, more damaging than the original offense. Jesus teaches that forgiveness is not an emotion, not forgetting or "getting over it," not necessarily reconciliation, and not necessarily relationship. He shows us how to stop the torture of both pseudoforgiveness and unforgiveness and how to allow him to unleash his love into our suffering with specific tools.

Next, Jesus and the woman at the well help us investigate the soul, the image of God in you, your identity in Christ, and the healing power of a sustained love relationship with Jesus. For Catholics, we drink from his love in the sacraments, scriptures, and Mass where that relationship is nourished through the Liturgy of the Word and the Liturgy of the Eucharist. Rather than judging ourselves for judging, we'll draw from the rich well of healing self-knowledge inherent in our judgments, thereby staving off worthlessness and other soul strongholds that block healing.

Then we'll consider how Jesus's love heals deafness to truth in the mind, where toxic lies stick, nest, and multiply in moments or seasons of neediness and deprivation. Do you also need to erect proper boundaries and learn to guard your peace? The biblical commands to "love your enemies" and "forgive those who trespass against you" do not include letting others abuse you. Abuse is sin; charity demands healthy boundaries for yourself and them (see Matthew 18). Healthy boundaries guard your gift of peace. We'll also determine how authority disorders and other strongholds block healing in the mind.

And finally, Jesus and the paralytic help us listen and attend to the Holy Spirit's way of communicating a need for healing, what needs to be healed, and even how to heal, through the body's physical symptoms. We'll discover how to outgrow destructive coping mechanisms. You know, like guilt. Shame. Sugar. Wine. You can't *control* destructive coping mechanisms. You know that by now, right? Let's learn new tools for coping and outgrow the destructive ones. We'll find help for body shaming and sexual wounds by studying the connection between the spirit and body with the Church, under Christ and in his Word. After identifying two main culprits that prevent physical healing, we'll learn tools to receive the healing power of God's love for our bodies.

How to Let the Healing Begin

So read this labor of love with an open heart. Here's the best way to do that:

Take your time. Healing is both an event and a process. You can't force a flower to open prematurely without killing it. Your heart is a sacred flower that opens fully under his love, and that takes time. But water and nourishment and warmth from the sun are "events" that help the flower open. Everything in nature grows slowly—almost invisibly—but inevitably under the right conditions.

Be gentle with yourself. "Love your neighbor as yourself." If you're ugly to your neighbor, it's likely because you have a habit of being ugly to yourself. Be at least as patient, gracious, and charitable with yourself as you know you should be with others' growth and healing. After all, the wounded "parts" of yourself are your first and closest neighbors, and they must be seen and heard in charity, too, for you to authentically love the neighbor outside of you.[3]

Do the work. Although it is miraculous, healing is not magic, and these tools are not magical. If God wanted to heal you completely and instantly of every spiritual, emotional, psychological, and physical malady, you would be in heaven. Although that might seem like an attractive prospect while you are suffering acutely, your capacity to give and receive love would remain eternally static at whatever point it is right now, and you would never again be able to merit a growth in your capacity to receive and give *more* love.[4] Not only that, but also no one escapes the necessity for healing; if we do not cooperate with God for healing here, we will still suffer the purification of our wounds in purgatory, without the benefit of the filter of a human body, a temporal support system of friends and family, or the sacraments. I will prove that to you later, but for right now, determine to *do the work*.

Even when Jesus healed miraculously, he always sent those he healed back into their lives to continue to work out their salvation. There are more suppressed, repressed, and hidden emotions, memories, judgments, places of unforgiveness, lies, and physical symptoms within you than you ever imagined, and they all need healing. Full healing occurs only in a love relationship with God, and relationships require time and work. They require discipline. Likely, you will experience major leaps forward in your healing as you read and practice the tools in this book, but as you discover yourself, you rediscover the wounds that sent you into hiding, and with those wounds comes pain, erupting from the deep. This is the work of purification and self-knowledge that the saints speak of, and it is a difficult "narrow road." But your promise is complete healing, and his Love is inexhaustible. There's always more! More love; more power; more of him. My spiritual director once said that the "narrow road" is more like a tightrope. But the work is worth it; you are worth it!

Prepare for transformation. Healing is the most important, purifying work of your life. As you heal, you break generational cycles of sin and woundedness. You become more you, the you he created you to be. Everything about you reaches toward full potential *and then some* by grace. The flower of you opens beautifully, spreading the scent of love everywhere.

Ask Christ for the revelation of self-knowledge as you consider yourself in him from so many love-angles. Implore him to touch and redeem your suffering through healing; to unite the fractured, scattered, wounded parts of you;[5] and to impress his healing love upon your dry, weary soul so that you are one with the most intimate secret of the Holy Trinity, the Suffering Servant, the Sorrowful Mother, and every Christian—past, present, and future—that has made this same glorious journey of love with him. For, as St. John of the Cross said, "in the evening of life, we will be judged on our love."[6]

It All Begins with the Heart

Psychological wounds and emotional pain occur and remain only in the heart.[7] So Jesus begins with the heart. We begin with the heart. An important qualification: there is nothing *wrong* with you. You do not need to be *fixed*. You just need to be healed. You just need love. Merely talking about or reliving memories never has and never will heal any emotional problem.[8] Only love opens hearts. Only love is permitted access to heart wounds, and only love heals them.

So, every wound, every sickness, every self-medicating and sinful habit proceeds from a lack of love or a deficit of love or a damaged love. You may be looking around worrying, "Where do I even begin? My marriage is a mess. My thoughts are a mess. My spiritual life is a mess. My finances are a mess. My relationships are a mess. My heart is cold and empty or trembling, or shriveled and fearful. Where do I start?"

The *Catechism of the Catholic Church* says that "to God all moments of time are present in their immediacy." God is I AM. He is now (*CCC*, 600). God loves you and desires communion with you *now*. Not when you *do* something, not when, but now.

HEALING IS Sacred

GOD wants to HEAL you.

LOVE is our primary NEED

When someone came to Jesus for healing, he has always healed

↘ He's interested in a relationship

a relationship of ← LOVE

The TRINITY is the most intimate secret of God revealed to us

God gazes across the Abyss and breathes life into it

LINE UP:
- heart
- soul
- mind
- strength

} So we can completely EXPERIENCE his LOVE

God LOVES us so much, that he came as human being to sacrifice himself so you could be healed.

He wants to HEAL you
↓
both an event and process

⇒ You don't irritate him with your neediness

He made you NEEDY.

He LOVES you and LOVE is going to HEAL you

One

Healing Is Sacred

The Great Commandment as Our Template for Wholeness

> And one of the scribes . . . asked him, "Which commandment is the first of all?" Jesus answered, "The first is, 'Hear, O Israel: The Lord our God, the Lord is one; and you shall love the Lord your God with all your heart, and with all your soul, and with all your mind, and with all your strength.'" (Mk 12:28–31)

I was in the car with my husband, who was driving us to the first location of a twelve-day, three-state speaking trip. We had never undertaken a ministry road trip together before, but all the upcoming event locations were in the South, within driving distance of our home, and my husband had left his day job the previous year to work with me full time. So, there we were, driving down the highway.

We hadn't been on the road for an hour when I got a call from my youngest son's school. I looked at the caller ID and my heart plummeted. I knew before I answered what awaited because we had been through this twice before. He had fallen behind and was probably failing something.[1] I threw up a prayer of frustration: *Really? Now? When I have to somehow put the issue to the side because I won't be able to address it for twelve days?*

When I'm preparing to pour myself out for your *people, as you've asked me to do?*

My suspicion confirmed, I disconnected the call and cried for the next thirty miles. He was seventeen, a senior, and had promised that he would ask for help when he got overwhelmed or did not know what he was supposed to do. That he wouldn't lie to my face and tell me he was caught up when he was behind a whole semester. At this stage, I could not and would not hold his hand and check up on him. He would either find the will to motivate himself or he would not, and I had made peace with both possibilities. But oh, the disappointment. And the anger! *What a* waste *of time, money, and opportunity!* I shrieked inside.

Thirty miles later, when I was sure I could do it without crying, I called him and confronted him, shortly and pointedly. My husband and I spent free time over the next twelve days discerning and deciding on consequences and how to otherwise deal with this cycle of misbehavior.

Because of my teaching skills and flexible schedule, my husband and I had agreed that I would bear most of the responsibility for educating our homeschooled kids. Our youngest was dual-enrolled in a classical online program for all of high school and was into his first two years of college. And because I was most familiar with the program and our son's abilities, I needed to decide what to do next. For sure, he would pay us back the full tuition for the class he had failed. And yet, somehow we needed to get at the heart of the issue.

I teach all the time that "twice makes a pattern." Sometimes that pattern is repeated in a single person—and sometimes from one generation to the next. Either way, these patterns can be opportunities for learning and healing.

The truth slowly dawned on me as I thought about the familiarity of the pattern. I had lost momentum during my senior year of high school and skipped eighty days of class. After graduation, I completed a year of college classes I liked and was interested in but then quit, forfeiting a full scholarship. *What a waste of time, money, and opportunity! How stupid! What an idiot!*

And therein lay the occasion to heal.

Although I later returned to school and remain a lifelong learner, I harbored anger at my younger self for floundering so aimlessly. St. John Chrysostom once said "sin is a wound,"[2] and one definition for the word *sin* is "forfeit." The Holy Spirit was using my son's behavior to reveal to me that I had a forfeit-wound from young adulthood. This wound needed healing—and I was largely clueless to that reality, because I was focused exclusively on how best to help and discipline our son. But when I recognized the Holy Spirit at work in the pattern, inviting me to cooperate with the healing process, I found an answer and, with it, a tremendous sense of peace.

After our trip, I had an appointment with my spiritual director, who pointed out that in childhood and adolescence my husband and I had been subjected to explosive and often arbitrary reactions from our parents when we made mistakes—reactions that we were determined our sons would not suffer. We had both tried to show restraint as parents—factoring in our children's personalities and temperaments and drawing wisdom from the daily readings to prevent our becoming too permissive. Still, my director said, receiving healing for this issue would also afford me patience and detachment regarding my son's choices and help me assist him without judgment and overreaction when he struggles.

In that moment, a Holy Spirit understanding dawned upon me. *If I wanted to help my son, I needed to figure out the source of my own anger. At whom was I really angry?* I squirmed in my chair under my director's silent, piercing look and was reminded of the first principle of hearing God speak:

When God speaks *to* us, he is speaking *about* us.

As Pope Francis taught in an address in St. Peter's Square, "Listening to God who speaks to us, and listening also to daily reality, [involves] paying attention to people, to events, because the Lord is at the door of our life and knocks in many ways, he puts signs on our path; he gives us the ability to see them."[3] The problem was not just my son's pattern of forfeit; I was residually angry at my younger self for having done exactly what he was doing.

This realization helped my spiritual director and me to engage productively in understanding both the problem and its solution. My director affirmed that my son was probably behaving this way for different reasons than I had, and he may have different needs than my own. And yet God was calling attention to this double pattern—his and mine—to point out a place *in me* that the Holy Spirit was attempting to heal. Only then would I be able to help my son accurately and dispassionately. Illuminated in spiritual direction, I opened my wound to the Holy Spirit, and he poured his love into it: *Lord Jesus, I ask you to take this anger from me and show me the* right *sacrifice; I ask you to heal the forfeit wound in my heart; I receive your healing.*

The Mystery of Love

Why is "love the Lord your God with all your heart, and with all your soul, and with all your mind, and with all your strength" the first and greatest commandment according to Jesus (Mk 12:30)? Because love heals. As we open the wounds we carry in every part of our humanity and personal experience to him, we are healed in each place, each hurt, each memory, each sad and tragic forfeit—however "minor"—through his love. This is the complete human healing God intends and performs (*CCC*, 1472–1473) in the fire of his love.[4] The *Catechism* explains: "God has revealed his innermost secret: God himself is an eternal exchange of love, Father, Son, and Holy Spirit, and he has destined us to share in that exchange" (*CCC*, 221). "Love is his first gift, containing all others" (*CCC*, 733). "He, then, gives us ... the very life of the Holy Trinity, which is to love as God has loved us" (*CCC*, 735).

The Holy Trinity is the most intimate secret of God. He exists in pure love, perfect relationship, and unbroken communion, and all healing proceeds from him, because all love proceeds from him. There is love available in your suffering, right now, the love of the Holy Spirit who is attempting to heal you through your patterns in relationships and circumstances. Because as St. John Paul II framed it in *Salvifici Doloris* (*Redemptive Suffering*), his apostolic letter on human suffering, "Suffering unleashes love." Why is that? Could it be because nothing exposes our weakness and vulnerability to us like suffering?

His Polish sister saint, Faustina, taught us in her *Diary of Divine Mercy* that God's mercy gushes forth to the lowest place, but only if we open it to him. Does he make us suffer so he can pour out his love? Or does his mercy automatically seek the lowest elevation in the soul, like Living Water?

Why is this "valley of tears" of life in the world so deluged with suffering? Because there is so little love in humanity that we are wounded to death from sin—our own sins and the sins that were sinned against us—and humanity has not yet learned how to open its wounds to him so he can unleash his love into them.

Love is the ultimate mystery, isn't it? Love is both the primary human need and the fundamental motivation of every human act: we're always, always, always either trying to get love or trying to give love. It's that basic. Marasmus babies (*marasmus* meaning "withered") showed us that babies with perfectly satisfactory physical care, who are not kissed and cuddled and touched, wither and often die. Marasmus was a condition prevalent during the late nineteenth century among babies in orphanages who didn't survive their first year; at the time, the babies were thought to receive satisfactory care but weren't loved.

Study after study bears out the reality that love is a more basic need than physical provision. The need for love is biological. The research of psychotherapist Arthur Janov proved that "love is not an abstraction but a literal neurochemical event."[5] In order to develop and grow, we *need* to love and be loved. *Every emotional, spiritual, and mental human pain and wound is ultimately caused by a deficit of love.*[6] Love is God's most intimate, healing secret, and he extends himself to pour it out in our suffering, as written in St. John Paul II's encyclical *Dives in Misericordia* (*Rich in Mercy*, 8): "The Cross is like a touch of eternal love upon the most painful wounds of man's earthly existence."

That wounded place in your heart is cold and empty; trembling and fearful and shriveled in the darkness; perhaps like Lazarus in the tomb for four days, it is dead and foul and putrid behind a heavy, painful stone, isolated and sealed off. "Jesus said, 'Take away the stone'" (Jn 11:39). He meets us in our suffering, but we must expose it to him.

Love like this is no casual endeavor, and Jesus is no impersonal lover. He calls Lazarus out of the tomb by name, and St. Augustine comments on this passage that if Jesus had not designated Lazarus by name, every tomb in the cemetery would have emptied. Jesus has experienced and communicates what our own contemplation of love is meant to teach humanity about God's presence and love *in suffering*. After all, "suffering unleashes love."

Have you ever noticed that, before he tells the story of Jesus raising Lazarus from the dead, the apostle John takes pains to point out that Jesus loved Lazarus and his sisters (Jn 11:5)? Over and over in the gospels, Jesus brings healing and wholeness to those he encountered—that is, he *saves* them—through love. The same love that brought them into being in the first place.

In your deepest wound, you are meant to experience this sacred exchange of Love that powers the universe, keeps it in being, and makes all things new. But how can you freely receive or give love when you're broken, resentful, and suspicious?

Where was Jesus then? Shouldn't I just wait for heaven to expect healing? Where do I even start?

"To God, all moments of time are present in their immediacy" (*CCC*, 600).

God loves you now, not "when you . . ."

Because God is I AM, because he exists in an eternal moment of love, healing is *now*. That's why Jesus never said to someone who came to him for healing, "Offer it up." Jesus healed everyone who asked in some place, some way, and some measure. He always heals. It's who he is. But even Lazarus's resurrection and life afterward prove *full healing is a process of love.*

Freedom from a Painful Past

Perhaps nothing in life is as excruciating as desperately groping for God's love to bring relief to our deepest wound, but still feeling abandoned in the pain of whatever happened "back there." Maybe you did it, maybe someone did it to you, maybe it "just happened." And yet, like Lazarus who was dead and stinking in the grave, we all do our best to perfume the foul stench of death with embalming spices, wrap such considerations in grave cloths, and put them away from us in the dark, in a cold, stone tomb of the heart. Sometimes we've had to bury someone we love. Sometimes we are the one buried, and can hardly bear to care anymore.

What's the point in rehashing it? we might reason. *It's long over. Everything will be fine one day. In heaven it will all be better.* But one day, two months, ten years come and go, and everything is worse and more painful because it was hidden away and never felt, never seen, never healed by love. *If the Gospel is such "Good News," if Jesus healed others, why hasn't he healed me? Why does nothing I do help? Why are my anxiety, my depression, my problems, my body, all sicker, darker, and more painful?*

Doesn't such suffering, whether throughout a lifetime or simply a season, make us yearn—*need*—to be stunned with eternity, like the three disciples on the Mount of Transfiguration? Don't we long to ache, instead, with the beauty that sears us in the weeping of violins; the silent, earthy creeping of dusk; the bliss of sloppy kisses and gangly little arms around a tired, disillusioned neck; for the awe we once felt from a black sky strewn with a billion stars and lit with ghostly aurora? How do we get from dead and buried to what makes us weep with the beauty of it?

Love heals. Love stuns. Love resurrects. Love renews. Love transforms.

The Great Commandment: God's Most Healing Secret

When asked by the scribe what the most important commandment was, Jesus answered with a daily Jewish prayer called the *Shema* (pronounced sheh-MAH), from Deuteronomy 6. Arguably the most well-known prayer in Jewish liturgy, the *Shema* is recited morning and night; in the final prayer on the holiest day of the Jewish year, the Day of Atonement; and, traditionally, as the last prayer before death. Jesus proclaimed the holy *Shema* the "first of all" the commandments (Mk 12:28–29), the primary law of God, and therefore the "fulfilling of the law" (Rom 13:10). "The first [commandment] is, 'Hear, O Israel, the Lord our God, the Lord is one; and you shall love the Lord your God with all your heart, and with all your soul, and with all your mind, and with all your strength'" (Mk 12:29–30).

Perhaps because it seems too big of an ask, or because God is invisible, we usually skip the first commandment and jump right to the second: "Love your neighbor" (Mk 12:31). That seems more manageable, tangible. I can do something about that. But *first* means *of primary importance*, and loving God whom I cannot see with all my heart, soul, mind, and strength seems impossibly comprehensive. The way in which the first of the Ten Commandments is worded is not merely something like "worship God only" but more like "love God with every cell, and thought, and emotion, and action."

Of course, "of primary importance" begs the question: to whom is such love primarily important? Is it God? Is God after your total self-donation of love because it's somehow good for him? Or could it be the primary commandment because he knows and wills that it is primarily good for *you*, the other?

Sin is a wound of love (*CCC*, 1853, 1856) in which the passions (emotions) become rebellious, the will is weakened and blinded by projections, the intellect (mind) is darkened, and the unity of body and soul is injured and made vulnerable to innumerable sicknesses and disorders, ultimately succumbing to the separation of body and soul in death. Sin wounds what makes us uniquely human among all matter and flesh—the ability to love God and to love others. It wounds or destroys our ability to receive and give love or even know what authentic love is, attacking God's own image in each of us, and through this attack sin opposes communion, both now and eternally, with God and with one another.

This is why the most relevant definition for sin is *destruction*. We are creatures who *need* relationship and mutual self-giving to grow and develop. The language of sin refers to those ways of living—thoughts, words, actions committed and omitted—that are destructive to authentic, mutually self-giving relationships. *If sin wounds love to this degree, then the first and greatest commandment to love God wholly must be the healing remedy for all love wounds.* Pope Benedict XVI agrees: "Whoever truly wishes to heal man must see him in his wholeness and must know that his ultimate healing can only be God's love."[7]

So, where do we start?

We start where the Holy Spirit is already working and inviting our cooperation: in our problems and suffering. Problems and suffering reveal the heart, the reservoir of wounded love (*CCC*, 1853).

Two

With All Your Heart

Jesus Heals the Blind... and Teaches Us to See

> They came to Jericho; and as he was leaving Jericho with his disciples and a great multitude, Bartimae′us, a blind man, the son of Timae′us, was sitting by the roadside. And when he heard that it was Jesus of Nazareth, he began to cry out and say, "Jesus, son of David, have mercy on me!" (Mk 10:46–48)

All three synoptic gospel writers relay the story of blind Bartimaeus (son of Timaeus), whose name means foul or impure (Mk 10:46–52). Imagine the scene with me.

There are no hospitals or doctors for degenerates like him, destitute and pushed to the edges of road and town. If his eyes are white with cataracts, if his hair and beard are a matted tangle, if the holey rags he's wearing reveal scabby elbows and calloused knees, well... consequences. The rumor is that his father once raped a Pharisee's daughter. And the religious leaders have always taught that all manner of misfortunes and physical illnesses are a result of sin, either personal or generational.[1]

The grime under his nails is visible when he waves in the direction Jesus is approaching. Jesus is why we're all here. Waiting.

Why couldn't he at least bathe?

Someone in the crowd hits Bartimaeus in the chest with a hunk of hard bread to shut him up, and smirks when it bounces and rolls to the ground. Bartimaeus doesn't grope for it. Instead, his mouth opens to cry hoarsely for Jesus through the feet of the crowd, and you look away with a little shiver of revulsion.

And just then, Jesus slows to a stop right in front of you both. Your heart skips a beat. Bartimaeus stares up, sightless, questioning, "Son of David, have mercy on me."

Jesus looks at blind Bartimaeus, who tosses his ragged tunic aside to stand before him on trembling legs. Then Jesus turns and looks directly into *your* seeing eyes.

"What do you want me to do for you?"

"That I May Receive My Sight"

The beggar lives every day with the obvious problem and suffering of blindness, and he wants to see. He wants an expansion of what he has physically known. He consciously seeks it from Jesus, unaware of his deeper, unconscious need for love. In his humility, he receives sight, the sight of Jesus standing before him with love, and he "follows Jesus" in a process of continual healing expansion in love.

In Bartimaeus's healing, the Pharisees, Sadducees, and scribes (religious leaders, lawyers, and academics) were confronted by a painful contradiction with their strong, previously held belief. Throughout his ministry, Jesus often pronounced that people's sins were forgiven at the same time as he healed them physically, because the Jews believed that sickness, death, disease, and misfortune were caused by personal or generational sin. This view was not "wrong," based on what had been previously revealed to them throughout Old Testament history and writings, just incomplete. But now, they were collectively ready for more complete revelation; the Messiah had come, and his revelation, if accepted, would "adjust" and increase what they had previously known in an expansion of deeper, fuller love. The healing of Bartimaeus's blindness was a conflict for the religious leaders, a problem meant to help them "see" something deeper, something *more*. We might call this conflict a "pop quiz."

But in typical human fashion, rather than evaluating the validity of their view within the evidence of God's love for Bartimaeus and themselves through Jesus's healing act, the religious leaders set about defending their unbelief by projecting it onto Jesus as heretical—maybe even evil—through a series of argumentative "questions." The narrative in Mark 10-12 presents each level of the Jewish hierarchy in the endeavor to discredit Jesus and protect their original belief. Jesus refuses to cooperate with their "blindness" and reminds them of the primacy of the *Shema*, of love.

We might say Bartimaeus, together with all the levels of hierarchy, represents all the parts of the human person that need healing: Bartimaeus suffers the pain of blindness—physical, emotional, and intellectual—and therefore *consciously* seeks to expand and see, while the Pharisees, Sadducees, and scribes who are *unconsciously*, inwardly blind and "in charge" block healing love through the distraction of insincere questions that seek to maintain their previously held view at all costs.

Can such contradictions exist in a single person?[2] Can such conflict lead to healing? Yes. Have you never questioned alongside St. Paul?

> I do not understand my own actions. For I do not do what I want, but I do the very thing I hate. Now if I do what I do not want, I agree that the law is good. So then it is no longer I that do it, but sin which dwells within me. For I know that nothing good dwells within me, that is, in my flesh. I can will what is right, but I cannot do it. For I do not do the good I want, but

> the evil I do not want is what I do. Now if I do what I do not want, it is no longer I that do it, but sin which dwells within me. (Rom 7:15–20)

The term "brokenhearted" in scripture means splintered or fragmented into pieces (see Isaiah 61:1), into contradictions and conflicts. The human person is full of conflicts and contradictions, most of which we are blind to until our "bad" behavior shocks us, or our suffering becomes so painful we can no longer distract ourselves from the truth.

After Jesus healed Bartimaeus, only one, a scribe, suffered the pain of conflict and contradiction long enough and consciously enough to probe deeper with Jesus so that he could "see" the love of God's heart and, in that love, see his own heart. Only he sought to remove the block to his own blindness and dug deeper into the meaning of blindness and healing by asking Jesus a sincere question that might cut through all the distractions: What is the "main thing"? Jesus answered with what the scribe already knew but had not yet entered into: "You shall love the Lord your God with all your heart, and with all your soul, and with all your mind, and with all your strength" (Mk 12:30).

Perhaps in the blind pain of your suffering, like Bartimaeus, you consciously seek only the relief of emotional or physical pain, but Jesus knows the need is deeper. He knows the need is healing in love. Not later, in heaven. Not when you get your shit together. Now. And the only way you might "see" that unconscious need is through pain. So, he allows conflict, pain, and suffering, because suffering reveals the heart.

Suffering Makes the Heart "See"

Psychiatrist Dr. M. Scott Peck proposed, in the first pages of his blockbuster book *The Road Less Traveled*, that depending on their severity, problems can provoke feelings that are dark and uncomfortable—at times extremely uncomfortable—such as rage, guilt, worthlessness, frustration, grief, loneliness, fear, anxiety, helplessness, and despair. These dark feelings may be every bit as painful as any physical pain, even excruciating physical suffering. And since life seems to present an endless series of difficulties, life is hard and full of suffering,[3] a university of love.

Despising and fearing the pain involved, most of us spend inordinate amounts of energy avoiding difficulties and inconveniences. We strategize; we force; we hurry; we project; we procrastinate; we deny; we self-medicate. Even when pain is unavoidable, we attempt to find an easier way around it rather than suffer through it fully in order to receive the promise of healing and love. But the substitutes inevitably become entrapments; the soul becomes sick and stuck and remains blind to love.

Was such blindness not illustrated in Eden? The serpent's temptation was to "see," that through distraction somehow their "eyes will be opened" (Gn 3:5). Adam and Eve could have possessed knowledge of good and evil without all the suffering if they had only "seen," acknowledged, and paid attention to the presence of the snake in the Garden with them and put the snake in its proper place, rather than allowing their attention to be diverted from the snake and onto the fruit of the tree.

We, too, can avoid the suffering inherent in distractions if we will only ask him to "see": if we will properly submit and take the darkness and blindness in ourselves to God in the gardens of our hearts. Whether Jesus healed the blind with a Word, a touch, or a process, healing involved seeing what was already there but was hidden or veiled; "seeing" involved an awareness of what was previously unconscious.

After the Fall, the only thing powerful enough to break through the blindness of our distractions and make us see is pain and suffering. If we can resist distraction and fully enter into that suffering with the Holy Spirit, we transcend it and heal. Because once we see the good in it, why he allows it, and that it is *not* arbitrary but intentional and purposeful for us, suffering is no longer simply bitter—it's *useful*. Jesus heals our blindness by using suffering to purify our unique wounds and help us see, because "whoever has suffered in the flesh has ceased from sin" (1 Pt 4:1). Habitual sin is blindness, a willing habit of distracting ourselves from "seeing" and participating in reality—the love wounds that exist in me and in every one of us.

This brings up an interesting point . . . why did Jesus go around healing people if their path to holiness entailed suffering? His *primary* purpose was to love—the *Shema*—and in love, to heal and save souls. Physical healings were a sign of a deeper, eternal love that was already being poured out into our suffering. When we work with him in healing our suffering at its root, "seeing," it ceases to be painful. Isn't that exactly what the saints say?

What Is the Heart?

The Bible often uses the terms *heart, spirit,* and *soul* interchangeably, while the Shema seems to distinguish between them. In addressing heart, soul, mind, and strength in this work—without introducing multiplicity—we might say the heart is properly the seat of the spirit, the image of God and reservoir of love of the human person. The spirit is the personality—mind and emotion: intellect, memory, and will. The soul is life-breath.[4] This is the Church's proper understanding of the "order" of the human person.

The great commandment begins with the heart, one's identity as image of God (love), and works outward to the body, not because the body is less important (never!) but because the entire human person behaves from and is affected most deeply and tragically by what injures the heart. I am following Jesus's outline. Although the delineation is somewhat arbitrary since they cannot be separated and overlap considerably, healing occurs most deeply and permanently inward to outward—heart, soul, mind, and strength.

Life is a constant litany of difficulties—and therefore a university of love—that even miraculous healing events do not erase. So, we must start where the Holy Spirit starts with us, in our daily sufferings and problems. Please keep in mind, however, that, biblically speaking, the heart is the seat of our love, the image of God; the spirit is the seat of personality, will, memories, and thoughts; the heart "contains" the spirit. The soul is the breath of life. In this work, however, we'll be using the term *soul* the way most of us use it now: to designate the part of us that worships.

Doctor of Prayer, St. John of the Cross, teaches that we must cooperate with the Holy Spirit in our suffering and "see" his hand in it to find its meaning for us, personally, because each individual's suffering is ordered to the healing of his and her individual wounds. Often these are wounds we received as children that result in a distorted view of God, as the Church points out.

> *The purification [healing] of our hearts has to do with paternal or maternal images*, stemming from our personal and cultural history, and influencing our relationship with God. God our Father transcends the categories of the created world. To impose our own ideas in this area "upon him" would be to fabricate idols to adore or pull down. To pray to the Father is to enter into his mystery as he is and as the Son has revealed him to us. (*CCC*, 2779, emphasis added)

A million Bible studies, daily church, "offering it up," years of therapy, healing services, multiplied deliverance prayers, spiritual direction, and coaching will never afford permanent relief if we continue to avoid our suffering and the Holy Spirit's message and love in it through blind distraction. We go from one holy thing to the other, finding short-term relief, but when suffering returns, as it must if we are to be wholly healed, we're left thinking it didn't work, we did it wrong, or that God must not have meant full healing for us. We *can* experience healing, and even further expansion in grace, when we know and respect God's ways.

Nature discloses that God's design for growth and healing is slow and gentle, repetitive, and seasonal, because we are limited creatures with limited immediate capacity for learning and experiencing truth. But deeper, more permanent healing is always available. Because God is "I AM," because he exists in an eternal moment, healing is now. So, we start with now. We start with the heart, where our wounded love resides. We start with our **pop quizzes**—the immediate, painful opportunities and experiences God allows to help us understand and identify areas of our woundedness. Pop quizzes offer an immediate path to healing because the Holy Spirit is continually offering them to help heal our hearts, souls, minds, *and* bodies.

Pop Quizzes Activate Suffering

Remember in school when the teacher would suddenly spring an unexpected test? "Time for a pop quiz!" It wasn't so much about the knowledge you'd gathered and maybe even memorized but whether you knew how to apply it. Not just *what* you'd learned but, in the day to day, to show if you knew how to use it.

Life offers us pop quizzes, too. Sometimes we get the pop quiz first, and then he expands our understanding through a homily, book, or something else; sometimes we learn something new from a spiritual conversation or conference, then we get a pop quiz to help us practice what we've learned. You likely had a recent pop quiz or will have one soon simply because you are learning about them. They're not punishment, but practice.

Pop quizzes are not simple, daily irritations, but inward or outward emotional eruptions that seem to come out of left field. The Bible calls them "vomit." "Like a dog that returns to his vomit is a fool that repeats his folly" (Prv 26:11). Sometimes they feel almost volcanic, and we explode. Sometimes they churn under the surface like molten lava, and we boil with shame, resentment, and bitterness. Our reactions to seemingly small things that people say and do are out of all proportion to the event.

Maybe you let someone have it. Perhaps you wanted to scream (or did). Or a torrent of tears seemed to come out of nowhere during lunch with your friends. Or you self-medicated. Again. Most likely, your reaction left you with feelings of shame or guilt. *What is wrong with me? "Good Christians" don't respond like that.*

What if I told you that your response probably had less to do with the situation, but was more a sign of where the Holy Spirit is already working to heal you and inviting your cooperation?

God works to heal us through these emotional eruptions that seem to come out of nowhere through conflicts in our relationships and circumstances that provoke the main heart wound. And because everything in creation repeats in patterns—tides, seasons, orbits, flower petals, human behavior—there's a pattern to them! The pattern of suffering in our pop quizzes helps us identify our main heart wound; the repetition helps us "see" that all our pop quizzes in every area of our lives center on this heart wound.

This is why we seem to encounter the same types of people, repeatedly, who do similar hurtful things that cause us to react in repetitive ways: someone hurts us and our main love wound is tweaked; we experience predictable physical symptoms, such as a tight chest or gut issues; we fall into a self-soothing sin habit, such as displays of anger or bingeing, or both; we feel guilty and ruminate on what bad people we are and *they* are, and can't stop thinking about the event and replaying it in our minds. See how pop quizzes involve the heart, soul, mind, and strength?

Pop quizzes cause pain in four areas: emotions (heart), judgments (soul), lies (mind), and physical symptoms (body). So they are *full* of self-knowledge that helps us "see," heal, and love more authentically in heart, soul, mind, and strength. As we gain practice in recognizing and working through them, eventually our pop quizzes coalesce into a recognizable "constellation" of symptoms in heart, soul, mind, and strength, like star-pictures that help us navigate and heal throughout our lives.

S.T.O.P.

We love the Lord with all our heart, soul, mind, and strength by cooperating with him in our pop quizzes; this is what I mean by "seeing." In the story of blind Bartimaeus, we are challenged to learn something important about how Jesus heals blindness: as we begin to allow Jesus to identify our heart wounds, the source of our suffering, the healing begins as he pours his love into them.

How, you ask? The way to work through pop quizzes fruitfully is to cooperate with the Holy Spirit using the STOP Tool™[5] from Psalm 4:4–5 (NKJV): "Be angry, and do not sin. Meditate within your heart on your bed, and be still. . . . Offer the sacrifices of righteousness, and put your trust in the LORD."

This four-step process is as follows:

S—Sin not in your symptoms, especially anger;
T—Tell God everything in your heart, soul, mind, and strength;
O—Offer the right sacrifice; and
P—Put your trust in God.

S = Sin Not

First, notice that anger is not a sin; it's a command. Be angry. Anger is a response to a perceived injustice, morally neutral in and of itself. It is said that St. John Chrysostom preached, "He who is not angry when he has cause to be sins, because excessive patience is the hotbed of many vices, and causes even the good man to do wrong."[6]

It's the way we respond in anger that can be sinful, whether we explode aggressively or boil passively. Part of the definition of "sin" is destruction, and both aggressive and passive anger are destructive. Aggressive anger is destructive to the other person; meanwhile, passive anger eats *me* alive in resentment and bitterness and makes me sick. I may even fall into passive-aggressive behaviors such as silent treatment or manipulation. Either way, the first step is to "see" our usual reactions and STOP before we react in sinful ways.

When we notice (without judgment) how our woundedness manifests itself in particular symptoms—you know, things like yelling, shame, migraines, self-medication, curling up in a ball and crying (my personal go-to)—we are able to look at those symptoms objectively, as though observing our own story like a fly on the wall, and strip them of the wound-driven, exaggerated emotion that's always present in the heat of the moment.

T = Tell God

Once you are aware, step two is to turn to your heavenly Father: Tell God everything in your heart, soul, mind, and body. Why? Because his "power is made perfect in weakness" (2 Cor 12:9). Historical emotions and reactions are automatically activated through your pop quizzes when a heart wound, usually from childhood, is activated. They most likely make you feel helpless—like you've actually hit rock bottom and there is nowhere else to fall.

And that is precisely where we finally find him and where he begins his true work in us, the love you were made for. Right there, in the wound at the bottom of the pit of vomit, is where he meets us with love and transforms that little bit of the heart, because remember, as St. John Paul the Great said, "suffering unleashes love." From the former Chair of the Pit of Vomit: Welcome, friend! It's only up and out from here.

But before we begin our ascent out of the pit, we have to address something. You've probably already started to feel it and pushed it down because you didn't like it. Imagine that I'm taking you lovingly by the shoulders, like a longtime trusted friend who loves you too much to lie to you, and I'm looking kindly into your eyes as I say: *Your pop quizzes are not about your husband or wife. They're not about your in-laws. They're not about your children. Your coworker, job, finances, friends? Not about them. They're about you.*

That probably hurt, so let it sink in and feel it for a moment. You need to be healed, so the Holy Spirit allows circumstances that provoke suffering in your wounds so you can see them and ask him to pour his love into them. That's the next step. Here's an important distinction, though: your pop quizzes are about you, but you are not a "problem." You are not a mistake, an accident, unlovable, or worthless. You don't need to be "fixed" either. You need to be healed.

Even so, perhaps because that's so, no one is responsible for your behavior and emotional vomit but you. It's totally natural to want to blame everyone else in your life for why your life is the way it is (projection, distraction, and blindness). People suck. I get it. But until we come to recognize that we are responsible for our behavior and emotions, our patterns of behavior and the hurts in our pop quizzes will continue beating us down.

Remember Psalm 4:4? "Be angry, but sin not." You can control the emotional vomit-spiral. You must. Your life is not a Disney movie, and no one is coming to rescue you from it. You can't cheat or shortcut your way through the university of love we call healing. "Be angry, but sin not" is a command. I'll show you how. But if you allow yourself to think everyone else is the problem, you get into the habit of believing there is nothing you can do to fix it. You will always feel this way, because the people around you are always going to be infuriating. When it's about you, though? It means that you can also be part of the solution.

But you are right, in a sense: because you're wounded, there is nothing *you* can do to heal it right now—except turn to the One who can. You likely don't even know where or what the main heart wound is. So that's why the next step is to take that whole mess of symptoms and drop it all into God's ready hands. I like to think of this exercise as holding the mess of all my symptoms in my arms like a precariously tall pile of laundry and plopping it down in God's lap with a hearty, "Here you go! How do we order this mess?"

Don't let misplaced fear of the Lord keep you from disclosing your heart; you needn't be mannerly or dignified in order to heal. The essence of communion (love) is complementarity: your weakness fits into God's strength; you love God *with your weakness*. Incredible, right? Almost too good to be true? This doubt is why so many of us do not experience his love in our hurts; we do not open our deficits and weaknesses to him because we are ashamed and afraid. He really wants the true you, not the "fake-holy" one. He will take the "fake-holy" and make it wholly holy. But not because you can't receive his love until you're fixed; rather, so your capacity grows to receive and give *more* love.

What are we "telling God" in the T step of the STOP Tool? We employ the T step by telling God everything we find in our heart, soul, mind, and body. In doing so, we love him in the four parts of the Great Commandment.

Heart, Soul, Mind, and Strength: The Shema

In healing the *heart*, two things that pop quizzes reveal to us are the *emotions* connected to a heart wound and the *memory* or memories attached to it. If you look back over your last three or four pop quizzes, you should see that even though they involve different circumstances, events, and relationships, they probably contain a strong common emotion. Don't judge it, just notice it.

Consider and remember that emotions are like puppies. They need to be trained—and they need to learn boundaries. When you get a new puppy and bring it home and into your house, what's the first thing he does? He pees on the floor! Does a good human mistreat or beat a puppy for peeing on the floor? He's a puppy. His bladder capacity is small, and he was not born with automatic control of his functions. But you don't want him peeing in the house and making a mess. So, you take the puppy outside and teach him through repetition and consistency to pee where it's appropriate and safe to pee, outdoors.

So it is with our emotions. All of them—the dark ones and the happy. They have to be trained and contained, because we don't want them making a mess of our inner and outer "houses." We observe such incontinent, historical emotions and work through them without condemnation or shame; we T—tell God, with whom they are safely and harmlessly eliminated, by working through our pop quizzes with him and in his presence.

So, tell God everything about the situation that you would tell to a friend or that you keep inside while pretending you're "fine." Get it all out: your feelings and thoughts about yourself and them; where you feel them in your body and what they feel like in your body; what the person said; what you wanted to say back; and what you want to do next, even if it's horrible, and even if you already did a horrible thing. Because he's God, you know? He already knows. It's we who are blind, so he wants *us* to know.

Let the puppy pee, then proceed to the heart.

How? Well, one way to do this is to keep a pop quiz journal and note the date, event, and symptoms. Don't worry if it's all a blur right now because a fight-or-flight reaction causes foggy thinking, and you'll have plenty more pop quizzes to help you discern further. Not comforting? It gets easier with practice, I promise, and eventually the emotional vomit disappears if you stay with the process. Really.

Ask: *What is the main emotion I am feeling? What is the memory behind this emotion and the symptoms I'm experiencing? When is the first time I can remember feeling exactly this way?*

The pain of your pop quiz should match the pain of the memory. You might see one memory or a series of memories; you may receive a picture, a single word (such as "bad"), a revelation of truth (that was not love), an inner knowing (yes, it happened), or merely a strong feeling.[7]

Once we have discerned the emotion and memory in the heart, we probe the *soul* for *judgments*, and we *forgive* "them" and ourselves; we discern the *lie* we came to believe about ourselves and them, and soak in the truth of God's Word for our *minds*; we explore the *symptoms* our *bodies* produce in the current pop quiz and the memory (or memories), and what information our bodies are communicating through those symptoms.

The soul, mind, and strength parts of the T step in the STOP Tool are in the following chapters. Right now, we are only looking at the heart part of the tool. The heart is where wounded love resides in damaged emotions and the memories associated with them. So if you receive few answers while searching for the emotion and memory in your latest pop quizzes in the STOP Tool, keep reading. I am leading you through your pop quizzes—heart, soul, mind, and strength—step by step, chapter by chapter. This is only the heart part, and we have three more to work through. At the end, I will give you all the steps to Working through Pop Quizzes in one concise place for future use.

Perhaps you'll find it as interesting as I do that the phrase "meditate within your heart on your bed" in Psalm 4:4–5 (NKJV), essentially the T—tell God step, is a Jewish reference to the recitation of the *Shema* before each night's rest. This dialogue with God is prayer—honest, messy, *real*. Maybe more real and healing than anything you've ever said to him before.

O = Offer the Right Sacrifice

When working through pop quizzes, we work on the heart or emotional part first, because the emotion is painfully and exponentially exaggerated due to a wound that's attached to a memory, often many similar memories. It's important to know and remind yourself of this truth when you're spiraling emotionally, so you learn not to overreact. Historical emotions activate the fight-flight-freeze response, so you will likely be irrational and incapable of thinking clearly. This is also why you shouldn't beat yourself up for "failing" a pop quiz. Fight-flight-freeze tends to disallow rational thought; rather, it favors panicky thoughts like "kill something," "get the hell out of here," or "hide and be still and quiet."

In fact, there's no way to fail a pop quiz. They aren't pass or fail at all but rather opportunities to see what we haven't yet seen and practice a different response to our triggers. They are a barometer that shows us how far we've come in healing and how far we have yet to go; that's all. *You cannot fail a pop quiz unless you refuse to work through what can be revealed in you by the experience.* Once your emotion has been diffused somewhat, *then* you can analyze, determine the right response, look for patterns and connections, and proceed to O—Offer the right sacrifice.

It sometimes takes a few days to work through a pop quiz completely, because the emotion obscures clear thinking while we're in fight-or-flight mode. My most powerful pop quizzes sometimes took a week or more to fully process. The time to heal is in the emotion; the time to analyze and do something ("offer the right sacrifice") is after the emotion passes. Else we do things in retaliation that we later come to regret.

What exactly do I mean by offering the *right* sacrifice? You might be thinking: "But Sonja, I *have* offered sacrifice! I go to church and receive the sacraments regularly. I offer my sufferings. I journal and read the Bible. I've done the St. Jude Novena, the fifty-four-day Rosary, the Litany of Humility, Consecrations, and the Surrender Novena. And nothing changes. I still feel angry, trapped, and hopeless."

Of course you do. That's what happens when you offer what *you* have determined a right sacrifice to be, rather than what *he* asks from you. As the scriptures say, "Has the Lord as great delight in burnt offerings and sacrifices, as in obeying the voice of the Lord? Behold, to obey is better than sacrifice" (1 Sm 15:22).

So, what *is* the "right thing" to do?

Start by praying: *Jesus, I ask you to take this emotion from me. I ask you to heal this wound in my heart. I receive your healing love. Father, in the Name of Jesus, our Healer and Savior, I ask you to send your Holy Spirit to heal every emotion associated with this memory in this moment. I forgive both my immediate offender and the offender in this memory, and I forgive myself, "for they know not what they do." I ask you to restore my heart and body, and bring new life into both, in Jesus's Name. Amen.*

Notice how you feel after that prayer. Has the emotion disappeared? If you still feel it, but it has lessened, pray again until it is gone. Perhaps you ask Jesus into the memory with you. What does he say and do?

When your emotions and body are quiet and still, you are ready to O—Offer the right sacrifice. Ask the Holy Spirit, "What is the right thing to do now?" "Offer right sacrifices" (Ps 4:5) means that whatever you and the Holy Spirit decide is the right thing to do in the situation, make a plan and do it. If over a couple of days you do not get clear direction in what to do, do nothing. Make resisting action a sacrifice and offer up your struggles.

No matter how many sufferings we offer up, if we have not discerned the healing message in the pop quiz, we have missed the whole point of why the Holy Spirit allowed it in the first place. Offering our own sacrifices in a pop quiz does not heal, because it leans on our own self-sufficiency and understanding (a no-no, according to Proverbs 3:5–6). Self-sufficiency causes clenched hands, pent-up frustration, and futility. It's like trying to reason with a toddler in a meltdown.

You've already found that offering up your suffering and multiplying your own sacrifices hasn't healed you or your habits or your relationships. It hasn't relieved the weariness of failure. So, what do you have to lose in trying it his way? When you just go through the usual motions in an effort to "get" what you want (relief) as quickly as possible, you aren't in the right frame of mind to receive his Word and will.

By allowing these pop quizzes, God *is* showing you his will. He's showing you where he is working and wants your cooperation, your sacrifice. Yes, it would be so much easier if he just pointed his ginormous finger and said audibly in a burning bush exactly what he wants you to do, but his goal is a *relationship* with you through which you can easily and automatically receive his healing love in your suffering. We do things his way, not our way, because he is the Way. But in his providence, God knows that we need to do a little bit of self-reflection work first. That's why steps one and two of the STOP Tool are so important, because we need to be in that frame of mind. And that's when he'll finally show you what to do next.

So even if you feel like you have offered the right sacrifice before, try it again. Simply ask him: what is the right thing to do now? Give him time to answer through the daily readings of the Church, through prayer, through your circumstances. And resist doing anything until you know for sure what the right sacrifice is.

P = Put Your Trust in God

Finally, put your trust in him. Leave the consequences and outcomes of your "right sacrifice" to him. Refuse the temptation to think about and ruminate over it anymore. For example, if you reach out to the person with whom you had a conflict and get a negative response, not a problem; you have done the right thing; the rest is up to God. Do not allow yourself to get sucked into a cockroach's nest of negative thoughts. (More on those in chapter 4.) As Our Lady put it, "Do whatever he tells you," and leave the results to him.

Healing is not a one-time event, except in death. Within the human person is an abyss of suppressed, repressed, and hidden emotions, conflicts, memories, judgments, places of unforgiveness, lies, and physical symptoms deeper and more contradictory than you could fathom, and they all need healing. Even when Jesus healed miraculously, every walking miracle still had to learn to "sin no more" and love authentically.

You will experience the thrill of walking with God; the weariness that comes from sin habits and lack of control will disappear in the power of God's Word in your life. But you need a long-term strategy. You will continue to experience pop quizzes, because you have been wounded deeply and repeatedly, and the Holy Spirit wants you healed just as deeply. He doesn't *cover* your wound with a robe of righteousness, like a towel over gangrene; he *heals* it inside out and scrubs out the stains (1 Jn 1:9). This is deep work; it takes time, and it's hard to yield to him when you're in pain or fear. But healing is your promise and inheritance in Christ. So, continue to work through your pop quizzes with him, using the STOP Tool, because love is why you're *here*.

Love Blocker: Unforgiveness

Did it feel like I glossed right over that forgiveness prayer in the O step? Nope. I waited to address it because, besides mortal sin, unforgiveness is the primary block to healing; it cherishes the offense and the pain rather than releasing and opening it to love. We will not be forgiven if we do not forgive (Mt 6:14–15). Unforgiveness is demonic torture, according to Jesus (Mt 18:34). It leaves the door of our hearts open to the enemy and gives him the right to torment and harass us with anxiety and fear.

Why is forgiveness so hard? Because it's a true sacrifice. But we have to know what forgiveness is so we don't fall into a toxic, pseudoforgiveness that prolongs our suffering by allowing others to continue to sin against us—a situation that can be more damaging than the original hurt.

Jesus compares forgiveness to writing off a debt (Mt 18:21–35). It's not a feeling, but a decision of the will; you're not saying the offense was okay; it's not forgetting (although we must not purposely remember and ruminate, as discussed in chapter 4); it's not allowing them to continue to sin against you; it's not even necessarily reconciliation or relationship. It's simply releasing them from the debt they owe you so that ensuing boundaries and consequences can be instructive and preventative of further harm rather than vengeful or retaliatory. When you forgive, you proclaim that they owe you nothing, not even an apology. You *expect* nothing, ever again. With your *will*.

Perhaps you're thinking, *Forgiveness! Bah! What about justice?!*

Forgiveness is part of justice, as scripture says, "If we confess our sins, he is faithful and *just*, and will *forgive* our sins and cleanse us from all unrighteousness" (1 Jn 1:9, emphasis added). I would even suggest that forgiveness is the supreme act of justice: "Mercy triumphs over judgment" (Jas 2:13).

We will discuss judgment and forgiveness more in chapter 3, but it's important to note, here, a gentle warning against spiritual-bypassing: saying we forgive without also working with the Holy Spirit to heal in heart, soul, mind, and strength. We cannot skip forgiveness and expect healing from God (Sir 28:3), but the opposite is also true: we cannot skip healing with a "holy-blanket" statement of "forgiveness" or we will stay stuck in pain, physical symptoms, and self-medication. We must forgive *and* heal. While you forgive with your will (not your emotions), the enemy will continue to remind you of the offense in order to suck you back into dark ruminations and pain. When he does, simply remind yourself that you already forgave the offender and continue working through your pop quizzes so that God can fully heal the wound. I like to visualize bringing the offender to the foot of the Cross and leaving them there. When the enemy reminds me of them, I remind him where they are! Then I can focus on healing, and discern if I need to erect a boundary.

The entire chapter of Matthew 18 outlines for us how to erect healthy boundaries before it speaks of forgiveness at all. It's not *either* forgiveness *or* boundaries; it's *both* forgiveness *and* boundaries. Both are a matter of authentic love. If they weren't, we wouldn't have the boundaries of the Ten Commandments or the *Shema* along with the forgiveness of sins. Love—charity—does not mean you must be a doormat, particularly because abuse is sin, and passively tolerating abuse makes us complicit in another's sin. If we are "forgiving" simply to overlook or evade healing and placing proper boundaries for ourselves or others, we are deluded about what both forgiveness and authentic love actually are.

While we're on the subject of authentic love, let's define it. Dr. M. Scott Peck defined love as "the will to extend oneself for the purpose of nurturing one's own or another's spiritual growth."[8] I like that definition because all growth is ultimately spiritual, and it's one of the best, concise secular definitions I have ever come across.

There are several biblical words for love that teach us about it, and we are meant to experience God in and through all of them. I am oversimplifying for brevity, but we might say *eros* is physical love; *phileo* is emotional love; and *agape* is divine, self-sacrificing love that treats others better than they deserve when it's in their best interests.

It's not in the other's best interests to allow him or her to abuse you or someone else. They need boundaries. It's not in your best interests to abuse yourself or others; you need boundaries. Healthy boundaries keep in what is safe and nurturing and keep out what is not. Boundaries are part of authentic love, as Jesus teaches in Matthew 18. Whatever improvements or adjustments we need to make to our boundaries,[9] using his teachings as our guide, complete forgiveness—seventy times seven—is separate and not optional according to Jesus's parable.[10] Both healthy boundaries and forgiveness are necessary for full healing and salvation.

Guilt and Shame Are Also Blocks to Healing Love

In my experience with over two hundred souls in one-on-one spiritual consultations, people have the hardest time forgiving *themselves* above anyone else. Long after receiving the sacraments, they writhe in guilt and shame; they fear God is as angry with them as they are with themselves; and they stay trapped in self-loathing, pain, and sickness.

According to the principle of first use, one way to understand what a word means in scripture is to study the context the first time it's used.[11] Guilt can be something like the soul's equivalent to the body's pain reflex, an indicator that something is wrong and we need to turn to God in repentance. But guilt is not from God when it's loaded with shame, condemnation, disgust, and contempt; such guilt and shame entered the human experience in the garden at the Fall. Guilt and shame are caused by sin, sins that we commit and sins that have been committed against us.

Contrition comes from God. Contrition says, "That was bad. Better not do that again." Shame and guilt say, "*You* are bad." Shame is about you and is inward focused as a form of pride, while contrition is about the "other" and is outward focused in love. Contrition is not loaded with judgment, contempt, and condemnation.

Contrary to feelings of guilt and shame, Jesus said, "For God sent the Son into the world, not to condemn the world, but that the world might be saved through him. He who believes in him is not condemned" (Jn 3:17–18). St. Paul is even clearer when he maintains, "There is therefore now no condemnation for those who are in Christ Jesus" (Rom 8:1).

How much condemnation? No condemnation. The same "complete and infinite" rules for forgiveness that we are required to apply to others must be applied to ourselves, else we make ourselves God and place ourselves above him (more on judgment in the next chapter). See how guilt and shame—condemnation—are accusations from the enemy, who is emboldened and entitled to harass and torment us through our failure to forgive ourselves? St. Julian of Norwich went so far as to say that God is never angry with us, because his nature is only love.[12]

I can almost hear you saying, "But Sonja, I *am* guilty." I reject that identity lie in the name of Jesus, because if you have confessed and if you have repented (meaning "to turn back" or "turn away"), you are *forgiven*. Even if you stumble repeatedly: "If anyone hears my sayings and does not keep them, I do not judge him," Jesus said, "for I did not come to judge the world but to save the world. He who rejects me and does not receive my sayings has a judge; the word that I have spoken will be his judge on the last day" (Jn 12:47–48). It's almost like he'll say at the end, "Didn't I tell you? Here's what I *told* you, but you wouldn't believe you were not condemned, and now look at all the love you lost and forfeited out of fear." What regret!

Once and for all, settle in your heart that guilt and shame are accusations from the enemy; they are attacks on your identity in Christ. The scriptures and saints are clear that the accusing, discouraging, condemning voice of the enemy must be ignored and fought, especially when we sin. Get up, admit your fault with contrition, receive the sacraments, and *move on.* Because unforgiveness against yourself is a grave sin that blocks healing.

Two Hearts Heal through a Pop Quiz

"Mom, something's wrong." My son's voice was dark and heavy at the other end of the line, uncharacteristic of his usually bright demeanor.[13] After a few minutes of conversation, I could tell that the weeklong irritability and melancholy he described was likely an unrecognized pop quiz.

I asked him when it started, and he probed his memory for the day the new insurance plans dropped at his wife's company. After two years of marriage and natural family planning, they were ready to begin having kids and had been looking forward to finding a suitable family plan for that purpose. But the plans were not as they had hoped, and the newlyweds had argued later that night about the necessity of postponing children a little longer, after my son had spent all day calling insurance companies and comparing alternative plans. He described himself in the succeeding days as angry over "every little thing" and depressed.

The main emotion underneath the irritability and sadness, he said, was "not-enoughness," and I knew we had hit the heart wound. The memory attached to that emotion was an altercation he and his father had when he was a teenager: he had come home late and had not completed a daily chore before work. When my husband got home, shortly after, there was a blowup after which my son left home for a week.

It was brutal for all of us. We all did soul-searching at the time, and I was convicted that my own criticism had also contributed to the ugly tear in the family. We recovered, and he returned home, but it had left a hurt in my son that was activated in the argument with his wife: he had done all he could do, and it wasn't enough.

Mercy, it gives me tears to write this, but as I listened to him pinpoint that memory and reexperience the pain of it, I prayed a dozen thank-yous to God for the privilege of walking him through the pop quiz and witnessing God's healing of a wound I helped create.

He located the "not-enoughness" in his chest; he was having a hard time drawing a full breath. He had thrown himself into fifteen-hour workdays in distraction. He had wallowed for days in self-loathing and criticism. I led him in forgiving himself and us. We renounced the lie that he is not enough and announced the truth that the Holy Spirit gave him in exchange for that lie: "I am enough for Jesus." He laughed with surprise when he received it, and my heart almost burst with love and gratitude.

"Do you remember when you used to have all those superhero dreams when you were little?" His "yes" came out squeaky through the emotion.

"You don't have to be Superman. You just have to be super you."

I suggested he imagine the little boy inside who just wanted to know he was a superhero and remind him that he was always "SUPER." We disconnected the call in order for both of us to recover, and I kept tabs on how he felt afterward. The darkness had completely lifted; he was back to the bright young man we all know and love so much; his wife texted me with shock and thanks that evening. He's been fascinated with pop quizzes and such since. Ha!

As we finish this chapter, the thought of exposing a bitter, withered, wounded heart to the omnipotent Creator might be a little unnerving. But be at peace. Remember that our heavenly Father loves us gently, slowly, with great tenderness. He sends his love in a little child, a baby in a manger.

You are also his child. You always have been.

Let's Review

- The first and greatest commandment is: "You shall love the Lord your God with all your heart, and with all your soul, and with all your mind, and with all your strength" (Mk 12:29–30).
- This primary commandment is a template for whole-person healing, because only love heals.
- I am blind to where I need healing; therefore, I need suffering to help me "see."
- I love the Lord with all my heart, soul, mind, and strength by cooperating with him in the pop quizzes he allows.
- I cooperate with the Holy Spirit in my pop quizzes by using the STOP Tool: Sin not, Tell God, Offer the right sacrifice, and Put your trust in him.
- In the T—tell God step, I begin with the heart. I love God with all my heart by allowing him to identify and pour his love into the heart wounds and memories hidden under the emotional suffering activated through my pop quizzes.
- Unforgiveness is a major block to my healing.
- Pervasive, long-term guilt and shame indicate unforgiveness for myself.
- I am his child. I am not condemned.

An Invitation

It's fascinating to me that Jesus emphasizes the beginning and end of his most comprehensive teaching on healthy boundaries and forgiveness between adult children of God by placing flesh and blood parables before him—actual children—and saying, "Let the children come to me" (Mt 19:14). Indeed. So let's do it.

Healing the heart is about memory and emotion. Whatever and wherever our painful memories and emotions from the past are, they influence our present and future through our inner child. You have an inner child. I have an inner child. We all do. Your inner child has a super-sensitive "antenna" that has been picking up messages way before he or she was even self-aware or able to fully understand or process events and emotions, mentally and emotionally. Your inner child holds emotions, memories, and beliefs from the past as well as hopes and dreams for the future.

Learning to love the demanding, controlling little you that still screams for attention and protection in your present and future can be challenging, but it is possible, and Jesus teaches it is necessary. Sometimes your hurt is too early to recall and can only be felt, as in womb experiences or preverbal, pre-self-aware implicit memory. Can we reach that deeply? St. Thérèse of Lisieux shows us a way, The Little Way. We become little again. Below is a technique called The Little Way Visualization, named after St. Thérèse of Lisieux's little way of childhood.[14]

Benediction—LOVE the Word®

L | Listen (Receive the Word.)

"And calling to him a child, he put him in the midst of them, and said, 'Truly, I say to you, unless you turn and become like children, you will never enter the kingdom of heaven. Whoever humbles himself like this child, he is the greatest in the kingdom of heaven'" (Mt 18:2–4).

To "turn" here, means to "turn back." We are going to humble ourselves before him and turn back to our wounded inner child.

O | Observe (Observe your relationships and circumstances.)

Part of self-knowledge is embracing the pain of leaving behind what was lost or never possessed, what is already behind and gone, that we blindly continue to cling to—consciously or unconsciously. No matter how good or how deficient our parents may have been, they were creatures, incapable of meeting our every need. It doesn't make them bad, just human. And yet, those childhood deficits remain painfully active in us as adults, provoking all our worst reactions.

Who or what did you need but never got as a child? What have you lost yet remain unwilling to let go of? What wound have you carried in your heart that you long for him to heal? How old were you when you received that wound?

Now, with all your senses, imagine you are walking through a lovely meadow of grass and flowers. You hear birdsong, feel warmed by the sun, and smell the earthy scent of recent rain on the breeze. Perhaps you feel the tickle of tall grass as you touch the dewy blades with your fingers. As you walk, you sense a presence beside you that is warm, strong, safe, welcoming, wise, and loving . . . it is Jesus who walks with you. Can you allow him to take your hand? As you walk with him, you see a figure, someone or something, becoming visible in the distance. As you and Jesus draw closer, you see it is . . . little you.

With Jesus by your side, you approach. What is your inner child doing? Does he or she see you? If she is reluctant, give her space; allow her to draw close when she is ready, letting her take comfort in Jesus's presence with both of you. What does your inner child need to hear and feel and know? Now, with adult hindsight born of experience, you can assure your inner child that all will be well. That she is safe. That she is good. That it's not her fault. That she is loved. That she is seen. That you are with her always, just as Jesus will never leave nor forsake either of you. You may express everything your inner child was not able to hear or experience or know as a child. Perhaps you draw her close and give her hugs and kisses.

When your inner child is at peace and you have said it all, when you are ready, visualize yourself holding your inner child while Jesus holds you. Feel the love pouring from his Sacred Heart into your heart, and from your heart into the child's heart. Stay a while in this love, she in your arms, both of you in his.

There are likely many wounded parts of you that were left behind at different ages that need your love and attention. Perhaps you may want to continue looking back for them, one at a time, until you have drawn them all into the warmth of your and Jesus's love.

V | Verbalize (Pray through your thoughts and emotions.)

Remembering that he loves you and that you are in his presence, talk to God about what you did or did not experience. You may want to write your reflections in a journal.[15]

Lord, this visualization made me realize . . .
I had difficulty with . . .
I am afraid of . . .
I need help with . . .

E | Entrust (May it be done to me according to your Word.)

Dearest Jesus, my love, in the words of little Thérèse, "For me to become great is impossible." Help me bear with myself and my many imperfections as I seek to follow her means of getting to heaven by a little way—very short and very straight—the little way. Amen.

Three

With All Your Soul

Jesus Revives the Woman at the Well . . . Why Judgments Can Help You Heal

> [Jesus] came to a town of Samar'ia, called Sy'char . . . Jacob's well was there, and so Jesus, wearied as he was with his journey, sat down beside the well. It was about the sixth hour.
> There came a woman of Samar'ia to draw water. Jesus said to her, "Give me a drink." (Jn 4:5–7)

She sniffs at the scorched sheets of Samaritan heat that billow up the hill almost supernaturally, even without wind to move them. A sunning lizard darts away from her next footfall, and she almost drops the ponderous clay jar with an irritated murmur. At least the tiny pebble wedged under the jug is no longer digging into her shoulder.

With her free hand, she tries to soothe the dehydration headache in her temples, but it still throbs in trepidation with each step toward rest and a drink under the terebinth tree by Jacob's well. She needs to get through the gauntlet of pretentious glares and whispers from the townspeople at the bottom of the hill in order to reach the well on the other side.

Snorting with contempt for the five useless husbands whose very existence force her to draw water in segregation, at the worst possible time of day, she pulls her veil farther over the swollen black eye given to her that morning by her latest paramour. The Torah says Isaac, Jacob, and Moses found wives at that marriage well, followed by innumerable men including her first husband, but she scoffs at the empty cistern of marriage that ensures, for most women, basic survival with little else beyond contingencies. So now she knows

how to dam a river of neediness,

how to wring priceless drops of hope from evaporated promises,

how to levee a stream of tears,

how to bear the aftertaste of a stagnant social fountain and splash her face in its shallow solitude.

Most of all, she knows better than to look for sympathy or understanding, even the most casual variety. She would never think of joining the company of other women at the usual dawn gathering for the day's water to share in their local gossip and news and laugh with them. It's not so refreshing when the laughter is at your own expense. She knows. That's why she's here at noon, alone, in her stifling headscarf.

Trudging up the other side of the hill, she hesitates when she sees a man leaning on the stone well by himself, looking her way. Somehow the cistern seems small beside him, almost as though he's propping it up. Is he waiting for someone? Briefly, she meets his gaze, then her eyes dart about at the emptiness around them. She puts down her pitcher. He's a Jew and she's a woman—a Samaritan—so neither of them will speak. But she needs water, and it's a long walk home with a full jar. So she shifts, needing to be left alone.

But not really. What she really needs is too deep and dry for words. She needs to be cherished. Suddenly, her empty clay pitcher feels like a metaphor for her life; she blinks away loneliness and shame, mingled with sweat, and wishes irritably that he would leave.

As though he heard her thoughts, he asks her for a drink. He looks her in the eye, searching her face; he questions all the destructive decisions that led to this significant well at this time of day; he reveals the drought in her soul.

The prophetic early rains have come (see Deuteronomy 11:11–14), and they feel like a fortunate flood of unconditional respect.

Love.

To her—a nameless woman trapped in another painful cycle of drama; whose leaders consigned her people to a history of idolatrous ritual worship of five Baals,[1] or "husbands"; whose stigma is as obvious as her black eye and perpetually unsatisfied thirst—Jesus offers the most profound discourse in scripture on worship and makes his first recorded self-revelation, first as a Jew, then "sir," and finally the Messiah, her true bridegroom, her living water. He pours love into her suffering; his mercy automatically seeks and soaks into the lowest elevation in her soul as soon as she opens it to him, gushing forth in living water.

Jesus diverted his route, his disciples, and the ancient religious and social enmity between Jews and Samaritans to drench this woman in a respectful love that would heal her abandonment, illuminate her projections, draw her soul into communion, and send her out to evangelize.

You are the Samaritan woman.

Idolatrous, but receptive. Sought out. Thirsty.

Like her, under his piercing knowledge of everything about you, you project: you fear your own worship is insufficient and does not or will not satisfy him; you're judgmental of yourself and those who do not worship like you. So you offer Jesus the distraction of a theological detour, and he redirects you to what will refresh your soul: love of God should not be an unquestioned acceptance of your parents' religious legacy, a dry, rigid structure of rules and checklists, or some shapeless private endeavor online or on a mountain or beach, but an ancient, ardent, free-flowing, *personal* love ceremony from the marriage well of truth.

Love Is the Alpha and Omega, Beginning and End

The entirety of scripture demonstrates and foretells this divine romance. The Bible begins and ends with love, with marriage, from Adam and Eve to the Marriage Supper of the Lamb. The Samaritan woman represents her people and all of us idolaters whom God woos away from loveless false gods in order to "marry" them (Hos 2).

From beginning to end, the Bible communicates God's love for mankind through a series of covenants, each one embraced and expanded by the next: with Adam and Eve at Creation, signified by the sign of marriage; with Noah and his family, signified by the rainbow; with Abraham and his tribe, signified by circumcision; with Moses and his nation, signified by the Passover "family meal"; with David and his kingdom, signified by a permanent throne; with the world through Jesus, signified by his Eucharist, his lamb's Body and Blood separated, multiplied, and poured out in the new covenant, given "for you" (1 Cor 11:23–26). The fulfillment of this final covenant will be the complete healing of the universe through him, our reigning king, signified by a new creation.

From the new covenant in his Body and Blood (1 Cor 11:23–26) flow the graces and power needed to heal the entire universe so that we can learn to return his torrential love in heart, soul, mind, and strength through seven sacraments, themselves covenants.

It's love, beginning to end.

Just like creation was declared "good" and "very good" from start to finish (Gn 1), the soul originates from God's love, is sustained in his love, is nurtured to maturity in his love, and returns to his love, so that there has never been a single moment of your existence that you have been unloved. You are loved so much, right now in our historical time, that Jesus says to you personally, "Go, your sins are forgiven." He reaches out his hand to touch you, literally, assuring, "Be healed. Love. I give you my Spirit and power."

When my sister was about five, she had a nightmare, for which our mom comforted her, "You don't have to be afraid, Jesus is here!" And my sister retorted, "Yeah, but I need somebody with skin on 'em!"

Before I came into full communion with the Catholic Church, I prayed a similar desperate sentiment: "Lord, is there not some way we can be *closer*?" Each of us longs for that literal, skin-on presence. However much we might doubt it possible, the need remains. It is this common need, this common longing, that Jesus addresses to the Samaritan woman—and through her, to all of us. "If you knew the gift of God, and who it is that says to you, 'Give me a drink,' you would have asked him, and he would have given you living water" (Jn 4:10).

Listen. "Give *me* a drink."

He is personally and literally asking *you* to do something for him, through which he will provide living water to you that will rush to the lowest place in your soul. And that something . . . is worship.

What Is Worship?

Essentially, worship answers the question, *How do I love the Lord with all my soul? What is the* most *healing direction to focus my love, my adoration?* To be sure, there are innumerable ways to worship. But there is a best, most healing way.

The first commandment is, "You shall love the Lord your God with all your heart, and with all your soul, and with all your mind, and with all your strength" (Mk 12:30), because nothing less than an infinite love will ever satisfy your infinite need for love. Because Jesus knew this, "he prepared [the Samaritan woman] to open her heart to the true adoration in Spirit and the self-revelation of Jesus as God's Anointed."[2] He prepared her to open her heart to him by guiding her to the self-knowledge in her judgments, and her acknowledgment of that self-knowledge led directly to a healing experience of his love that corrected her incomplete ancestral worship and inspired her adoration. Why? Because "it is the greatest of all disciplines to know oneself; for when a man knows himself, he knows God," taught Clement of Alexandria.[3] Proper worship loops us back into his love, which continues to heal and inspire our worship and bring us closer to him in love.

Loving the Lord with all your soul—God-first worship—is not about God receiving anything from us and our adoration. Jesus doesn't want something *from* you; he has something *for* you. Every soul is feminine in relationship to God, because God is always Giver and the soul is always receiver. We add nothing to him with our worship. He doesn't need our love or worship. *We* need *him* for love in worship. Adoration of God heals us.

Man is not a pure spirit but is composed of body and soul, and his basic need for love requires that he should adore God not only in his soul but also in his body.[4] This is the justification of all external manifestations of worship—genuflection, prostration, kneeling, standing, the Sign of the Cross, the lifting-up or imposition of hands—in rendering to God the honor due to him. Worship is not an optional act of the creature; God is entitled to the worship of intelligent creatures as a matter of justice and their inherent needs.

Spirituality is not some emotional "opiate of the masses," as Marx declared it, but has been hardwired into humanity. It's a biological need for love that requires an outlet for us to thrive. One study demonstrated that adolescent depression and spirituality are two sides of the same coin, so that if an adolescent's spirituality is not directed so that it comes "online," he has an

80 percent chance of becoming depressed.[5] God loves humanity first; therefore, our primary need is love, and the need to worship precedes us in every civilization.

When we worship, God is not an egotistical tyrant waiting to judge us for perceived infractions. So why is "love God first and best and highest" the first commandment and part of the *Shema*? Because proper worship is love that *heals*.

He knows what type of worship is *best* for us, so he reveals and communicates it—first to the Jewish people through Moses with the Tabernacle; then in the prophets with the Messianic Temple (a prophetic vision of the Church, particularly in Ezekiel 44); then through Jesus and the apostles; and finally, he shows how worship is occurring in eternity through John's Apocalypse, so that conformance will lead into the intimacy and familiarity of heaven.

The worship God prescribes throughout the entire scope of biblical revelation is ceremonial, hierarchical, liturgical (meaning a "work of the people"), temporal (for us, rooted in physical space and time), sacrificial, and priestly. It's sacramental and purifying, communicating grace; it's sensory and whole body; it's communal; it's transcendent, connecting us with people of faith in the past, present, and future; it "*presents*."[6]

Proper worship, according to the entirety of scripture, is the gift of God, a present in which he is present, touching and healing: "If you knew the gift of God, and who it is that is saying to you, 'Give me a drink,' you would have asked him, and he would have given you living water" (Jn 4:10).

The Sacraments Are Jesus's Healing Presence

Have you ever read about Jesus's healing miracles in the gospels and wished *you* could be there, hearing his healing Words in your ears, physically feeling his healing touch on your skin, and experiencing tangible healing? Why did Jesus only heal publicly for three years, heal such a small group of people, and then leave, if his healing ministry was to be a universal promise to all of us? Where is Jesus's public ministry now? How can I access the literal, physical love of Jesus today?

In the sacraments.

Perhaps it's so basic we've forgotten: the sacraments bring the public healing ministry of Christ's love for us into the present. They are Jesus healing in person, offering us living water from the marriage well of eternal love.

St. Augustine said the sacraments are outward signs of inward grace, instituted by Christ for our sanctification.[7] We can also say that the sacraments are outward signs of inward *love*. In Greek, the main original language of the New Testament, the words *karis* ("grace") and *agape* ("love") are closely related, as in 1 Corinthians 13. This passage is often called "the love chapter," and the word *love* is often translated "charity," from the Greek word *karis*. So we can say the sacraments are communications of love. Because love heals.

In his book *Be Transformed*, Dr. Bob Schuchts outlines how the sacraments heal specific wounds. Baptism heals rejection wounds by making us God's children, Communion heals abandonment wounds through Jesus's Eucharistic presence, and Confirmation heals powerlessness wounds though the gift of the Holy Spirit.

Dr. Schuchts separates Holy Orders and Matrimony by the wounds addressed in their sacramental graces, but those wounds and graces act upon the receivers of both sacraments in similar ways, since Catholic priests are "married" to the Church, while husbands are "head of" their wives in a miniature hierarchy (Eph 5:23–24). Therefore, these two sacraments respectively heal authority wounds through establishment of proper order and wounds of fear and mistrust through faithful, authentic love relationships.

Confession heals shame and restores single-hearted love; Anointing of the Sick, also part of Last Rites, primarily heals hopelessness and fear of death, but can also heal physical symptoms. Through the covenants and sacraments of the new covenant, we enter into and participate in a formal love-oath, an eternal "exchange of persons" with God (an explanatory phrase for "covenant" often used by Dr. Scott Hahn) that addresses the entire human person throughout his life unto ultimate healing in, with, and through love.

As a former Southern Baptist, even after twenty years as a Catholic I am continually enthralled by the supernatural power of the sacraments to order, heal, and empower my life. Called to public ministry in my twenties, I threw myself into pursuing him with a single-mindedness and exhilaration that marginalized even my marriage and kids. As a stay-at-home mom, I relished my spiritual gift of teaching, regularly studying the Bible on my own and in seminary classes forty-plus hours a week. I would study all day and then realize it was almost time for my husband to come home from work, and I hadn't taken a shower or brushed my teeth, started dinner, or done any chores. I would scramble to catch up before he arrived to find the chaos at home, excusing myself with the thought that I was following Jesus single-mindedly, and wasn't that what every Christian is called to do? How can you do too much for Jesus?

Sadly, as a Baptist, I had seen this carelessness modeled for me by almost every pastor and ministry leader I knew. It was a well-known joke that preachers' and deacons' kids (PKs and DKs as they were called) were some of the most emotionally unstable and worst behaved because leaders almost always prioritized the needs of ministry over their personal relationship with God as well as over their own needs and those of their families. And although, admittedly, the extent of my knowledge was limited, I never met a preacher's family that appreciated being so far down the priority list.

It wasn't until I began my journey into the Catholic Church and was exposed to her teaching on vocations and vocational priorities, particularly in *Apostolicam Actuositatem* (*The Decree on the Apostolate of the Laity*) by Pope Paul VI, that I fully realized my error; subsequently, my family and I were healed of my own ignorant insensitivity to authentic love. Although I had felt the Lord correct me for overzealousness and adjusted the time I spent reading, studying, and praying, I never really understood why he had corrected me and always felt a little guilty for it, even while also experiencing relief that I could freely give more love and attention to my family.

Learning from the Church to properly prioritize the demands of my vocation was instrumental in helping me serve in the proper hierarchy of worship for my active and married life:

- our primary vocation is to God himself, our personal relationship to personal, Trinitarian Love;
- our secondary vocation is whatever sacramental vocation we are called to (mine is marriage and family); and
- *then* one's "call within a call," as Mother Teresa framed it, is to our work, apostolate, or ministry.

This same hierarchy of priorities is outlined in the order of the Ten Commandments: God first, then family, then everything else. I needed the Church's authority structure and its teaching through the Magisterium—made up of those ordained through the Sacrament of Holy Orders—to help me reorder my view of the Sacrament of Marriage according to authentic love that takes everything into account: my relationship with God, my family, my own healing, and the healing of those whom I hope to serve.

Within the Sacrament of Marriage, I could also clearly see the call to proper order that St. Paul speaks of in Ephesians 5—Jesus, then the husband, then the wife, then the children—not as some patriarchal power play but as a natural reflection of the hierarchies in creation and the Church herself.

For many of us with authority wounds (particularly mother or father wounds), the prospect of offering loving obedience to God, let alone any human being, is not easy or fun. And yet that is exactly where the healing begins, as we struggle to show our love for the Lord through obedience to those in authority over us in the Christian life. "If you love me, you will keep my commandments" (Jn 14:15). How could anyone manage to love Jesus through obedience to those in authority without grace?

Thankfully, the sacramental graces of the Eucharist are specific to charity, or authentic love. In the Eucharist, Jesus's love increases the purity of our love and our capacity and ability to love. Anytime I feel unable to conquer a particular vice, such as rebellion (anyone else?), I increase the frequency with which I receive the Eucharist;[8] it is the healing food that eclipses and conquers Eve's "apples" of distraction. But more than that, for me it was the answer to my prayer to be *closer* to God. The Eucharist is a mystical Body-to-body super-marital union of love that heals us of abandonment and other love wounds *in the context of* the love deficits inherent in our individual secondary and tertiary vocations.

Love Blockers: Disorder and Rebellion

We cannot love properly with all our hearts, souls, minds, and strength when our authority structures are disordered or we are in open rebellion against them, because God created all things in hierarchies and in order. Order is necessary for our spiritual protection and safety, so that his love to us flows freely and our love to others is also unobstructed by spiritual crookedness or iniquity. The love we are able to receive amid a disordered authority structure is necessarily limited because the pipeline of love has a structural kink in it.

My own healing and ability to love, and that of my entire family, increased dramatically by placing myself under the authority of Jesus's Word and ministry in his ancient Church through her teachings and sacraments. Additionally, hundreds of one-on-one consultations have convinced me that authority and priority disorders (two sides of the same coin) block healing.

Scripture is clear that proper worship involves receiving Jesus's sacramental love through proper authority structures that facilitate the free-flow of living water that heals the soul. The soul heals in that love to the extent that we access it through the sacraments as we work through the suffering in our pop quizzes.

What Is the Soul?

Although the human body issues from the procreative union of physical parents, "the soul is created immediately by God" and is the "form of the body" (*CCC*, 365–366), meaning its substance. This is why anxiety that is based on fears of existence (something bad will happen, I'm in danger, I'm going to die) often proceeds from a mother wound,[9] according to research. Mother gives birth to me, so mother equals earthly existence. The healing answer to such anxiety ultimately lies before mother, in God, through whose love we are first brought into existence as "fearfully and wonderfully made" (Ps 139:14, KJV).

"Fearfully" in this translation means respectfully, with creativity, forethought, deliberation, and love. Although woundedness can unbalance them, the essence of your personality and temperament (along with your gifts and talents and interests), can never be "too much" or inadequate, because you were created with careful intention and "wonder" (Ps 139). In fact, St. Thomas Aquinas teaches that all things proceed from and continue being in Love, or they would cease to exist. It's a reality that moved St. Paul to write, "In him we live and move and have our being" (Acts 17:28). The Book of Wisdom elaborates:

> For you love all things that exist, and detest none of the things that you have made, for you would not have made anything if you had hated it. How would anything have endured if you had not willed it? Or how would anything not called forth by you have been preserved? You spare all things, for they

are yours, O Lord, you who love the living. For your immortal spirit is in all things. (Ws 11:24–12:1)

Is there any doubt, then, that we are loved? Always have been, from conception, and always will be, beyond death? We are called to a full self-donation of love that heals the soul and inspires true healing, universal worship, and communion. After all, "the one who strives for self-knowledge, like the woman at the well, will affect others with a desire to know the truth that can free them too."[10] The covenants, sacraments, and hierarchies all communicate the reality of this love, and Jesus directs us through the Samaritan woman in another, perhaps unlikely, way we can receive it.

Pop Quiz: "Give Me a Drink"

The sacraments are unique conduits of God's healing love; therefore, proper worship through them is ultimately best for us. But for all that, worship is not self-centered. Worship is a *relationship,* an exchange of full, self-donating love that is wholly God-directed.

Woundedness and suffering seem to obscure our experience of God's love (see *Salvifici Doloris* [*Redemptive Suffering*]), sometimes even while we're participating in the sacramental economy. Pain causes us to turn inward in self-protection and projection; self-protection and projection lead to self-worship. Therefore, the Holy Spirit offers us pop quizzes to help us see them and receive his healing love in our projections.

In contrast to blind Bartimaeus, a Jew who freely asked to see, the Samaritan woman is too tyrannized by both religious and feminine shame to reveal her vulnerability to anyone, too sorrowful to ask for healing, too blinded by projections to even know what to ask for or where to begin. Jesus sees this, and his gentle engagement with the woman is intended to draw her out toward the reality of her situation.

As a Samaritan, the woman's soul is necessarily withered from worshiping five Baals (husband-gods) out of a historical deficit of proper hierarchy and truth, as Jesus points out to her.[11] After six men, she likely carries a deep trauma, a deep wound of worthlessness that prevents her from experiencing God's love and mercy. Dare I say that Jesus initiates a pop quiz for this woman by probing those wounds?

He begins with a command and assertion that surely felt abrupt and pointed: "Give me a drink.... If you knew the gift of God... you would have asked him, and he would have given you living water" (Jn 4:7–10). He knows she is thirsting to death but doesn't know who or what to ask for, so he asks *her* for a drink, drawing her out in service to him that ultimately inspires her worship and satisfies his thirst for her love.

He deliberately points out that she doesn't know the gift of God; he purposely highlights that she doesn't know his love, that she can't ask for relief because she doesn't know she can nor how to receive it. What she's been taught is too incomplete. She no longer looks to a man or tacit religion to save her; she knows better from all the pain she's experienced with both. Jesus's statements seem to activate a pop quiz that makes her *feel* the gaping dryness and emptiness of it all. We know because she responds with cynicism: "How is it that you, a Jew, ask a drink of me, a woman of Samar'ia?" She relates with sarcasm: "Are you greater than our father Jacob...?" She reveals a judgment: "Our fathers worshiped on this mountain; and you [Jews] say that in Jerusalem is the place where men ought to worship" (Jn 4:9, 12, 20).

Neither Jesus nor the woman is at this well for water; he's thirsty for her love because she is thirsty for his. In preparation for living water, Jesus blows the dust off her wounds and cynicism: "Go, call your husband" and "You worship what you do not know" (Jn 4:16, 22).

Under this same type of painful exposure of our deficits, perhaps we, too, wither in our pop quizzes, where all our hurts and judgments come leaping to the surface like spawning salmon.

Maybe we even whine, *Why are you* doing *this to me?!* In cynical ignorance of the spiritual value of pop quizzes, we might even become habitually sarcastic in speaking of ourselves and others whom we judge. But cynicism and sarcasm often indicate a soul subconsciously shriveled up as it sits in the seat of judgment or self-worship.

Judgments, then, are a rich source of self-knowledge that we ask the Holy Spirit to reveal in the T step, in the soul part of a pop quiz. They proceed from the lowest place of the soul and therefore attract Jesus's love and mercy. That is, they are a rich source of refreshing, renewing self-knowledge *if* we can refrain from judging ourselves for judging!

Judgments Reveal My Object of Worship

St. Augustine points out, "Men are hopeless creatures, and the less they concentrate on their own sins, the more interested they become in the sins of others.[12] Unable to excuse themselves, they are ready to accuse others." Every human being projects his faults and inferiorities onto his neighbor and is continually offended by them. Therefore, Jesus teaches,

> Judge not, that you be not judged. For with the judgment you pronounce you will be judged, and the measure you give will be the measure you get. Why do you see the speck that is in your brother's eye, but do not notice the log that is in your own eye? Or how can you say to your brother, "Let me take the speck out of your eye," when there is the log in your own eye? You hypocrite, first take the log out of your own eye, and then you will see clearly to take the speck out of your brother's eye. (Mt 7:1–5)

In this passage, Jesus is not pronouncing that he will accuse us with our own judgments; *he is revealing that judgment is not imposed from the top down.* We judge ourselves but project our own inferiorities onto our neighbor, accusing him secretly or openly. Judgment begins from the bottom of the soul and moves up and out as projection, and we are allowed to keep such condemnation of ourselves unto eternity if we continue in the lack of love and mercy that stubbornly maintains it.

We cannot bear to see our own inferiorities, so we cast them away from us while seeing them clearly in others; when we do see them in ourselves, we wallow in shame and guilt, which are self-accusation and self-judgment—all self-worship. Remember from chapter 2 that "there is therefore now no condemnation for those who are in Christ Jesus" (Rom 8:1)?

> I have come as light into the world, that whoever believes in me may not remain in darkness. If any one hears my sayings *and does not keep them*, I do not judge him; for I did not come to judge the world but to save the world. He who rejects me and does not receive my sayings has a judge; the word that I have spoken will be his judge on the last day. (Jn 12:46–48, emphasis added)

We are judged in the measure and with the same measure that we judge, because we take it upon ourselves to play God with ourselves and our neighbors in deciding who or what is good and bad, rather than simply experiencing life and learning to love through it as it comes. Again, *judgment* as we are discussing it here is not the detached observation or evaluation that we are called to and that orders things properly in love but an observation or evaluation containing contempt, disgust, accusation, cynicism, and condemnation that makes us blind and unable to order or love properly. In the end, God allows us to keep whatever we have chosen, condemnation (self) or love (him).

"Judge Not . . ."? What About the Judgment?

Doesn't the truth of "no condemnation for those in Christ" seem almost too good to be true? But wait . . . so does everyone just get away with sin, even horrific sin? If there's no condemnation, what is the nature of Judgment Day?

First, no one gets away with any sin, because "one is punished by the very things by which he sins" (Ws 11:16). Judgment for sin is chosen along with the sin, because wrath and judgment are built into sin the way gravity is built into the cosmos. If you step off the Empire State Building, your skull splits open like a melon. Is the ground mad at you? Is gravity condemning you? Is the mess you're left with some sort of personal revenge for transgressing the law of gravity? No, it's a natural law containing inherent accountability!

There are spiritual laws, too: "The wages of sin is death" (Rom 6:23). Sin will kill you. But Jesus took on our condemnation for sin, defeated it, and is no longer condemned, so we who are "in Christ" aren't either. He is resurrected, so we are, too: "The wages of sin is death, but the free gift of God is eternal life *in Christ Jesus our Lord*" (Rom 6:23, emphasis added).

Remember that justice is for the unrepentant; mercy is for the repentant. We should pray for the grace of illumination of our judgments, so we have the opportunity to repent of them and receive God's mercy. Because at Judgment Day, all of our projections will be revealed to us, as will the persistent, all-consuming love of the Father that Jesus told us all about and modeled at the Cross. At that point, the Great I-Told-You-So will commence: "The word that I have spoken will be his judge on the last day" (Jn 12:48).

Experiencing and realizing that we have always been held in this pure and subsisting love, we will be in terrible pain to see how selfishly, stubbornly, blindly, and fearfully we judged—ourselves first, then everyone else—all while we have been loved and freed completely and told all about it. But we will maintain for eternity the same capacity for love with which we died. In the evening of life, we will be judged on our love, according to St. John of the Cross.[13] "Therefore do not pronounce judgment before the time, before the Lord comes, who will bring to light the things now hidden in darkness and will disclose the purposes of the heart. Then every man will receive his commendation from God" (1 Cor 4:5).

With perfect accountability and agreement, many, many, many will see the heinous lack of love they have lived from and persisted in toward themselves and others. They will see and acknowledge in totality their blind projections and wounds and errors and evil and weakness; they will then experience and understand the full potency of their shame, guilt, fear, and rage; but they will not experience or understand mercy, because the darkness they continually chose cannot comprehend or apprehend it (Jn 1:5). At the extreme, they will agree their evil requires justice, and because they will have known nothing of mercy and lived with no mercy, they will flee his presence having refused to trust in his mercy.

Therefore, Jesus's Words will prove true: "He who rejects me and does not receive my sayings has a judge; the word that I have spoken will be his judge on the last day" (Jn 12:48). What a travesty to stand before the One who suffered and died for love of us and say to his beautiful face, "I am not worthy of love; I do not know mercy; I cannot receive your mercy; I will not." Yet this is how most Christians live right now, wallowing in guilt and shame and unforgiveness for oneself, which is then projected onto the neighbor, and even onto God himself! If we worship ourselves by presuming to condemn ourselves and others, we are left with condemnation, because God has made free will absolutely inviolable.

We see this further illustrated in Matthew 18, where the servant who has been forgiven a debt he could never repay demands repayment for a tiny amount from a fellow servant. Why does he do that? Because he cannot receive forgiveness for himself. The debt is gone, but he projects his shame and guilt onto his fellow man. Jesus calls this projection of unforgiveness demonic torture: "The master handed him over to the torturers until he should pay all his debt" (Mt 18:34, NJB).

It seems to me that judgment is a woefully overlooked disorder of the Fall. As soon as Adam and Eve sinned, they began judging and fearing God with suspicion of his motives, his goodness, his continuing love for them, and his trustworthiness. But it was they who began hiding, judging themselves in overwhelming shame, condemnation, and fear. They became, in the framing of Dr. Jordan Peterson, "self-conscious,"[14] hiding behind projections against one another and God himself. But just as quickly, God pronounced the coming redemption operation in the protoevangelium (see Genesis 3:15) and provided temporary cover for their nakedness with a blood sacrifice.

In contrast, in her *Dialogues*, St. Catherine of Siena professed that we love others with the same intensity and passion with which we feel loved by God. If we are full of love deficits, doubtful of God's love for us, and brimming with self-condemnation that we project onto God and others, how can we love anyone at all, and who wants to get close to us?

We were created to experience everything God gifts us with for pleasure, work, and relationships and to learn to love better and more authentically through it all. But after the Fall, the darkness and blindness of our judgments became so inherent in humanity, so suppressed and repressed in the subconscious, that it takes an act of God to reveal them to us through other people: "One meets with projections, one does not make them. . . . Projections change the world into the replica of one's own unknown face."[15]

The Samaritan woman's pop quiz exposed a projection about proper worship, and Jesus illumined it with his Word without judgment for her. Similarly, we must seek to see the projection of our deficit of love in our pop quizzes with the Holy Spirit and allow him to reveal and renew us in his living water, the sacraments.

Love Blocker:
The Spirit of Accusation

"Father, forgive them; for they know not what they do" (Lk 23:34). Jesus prayed this from the agony of the Cross. Words of unfathomable mercy. Was he speaking of the Jews or the Romans? Did they really not know what they were doing? St. Paul says none of the rulers knew, "for if they had, they would not have crucified the Lord of glory" (1 Cor 2:8).

But how could they not know? Even if we excuse their lack of understanding that Jesus was God, despite his miracles and the divine wisdom of his teaching, how could anyone not know that torturing and murdering another was not right? How could anyone believe that sort of cruelty was okay?

Blindness. Projections. They drive us subconsciously. Despite the miracles and wisdom of Christ, they couldn't stop themselves from judging and hating him. They believed they were actually reflecting God's own "justice" and "anger" in *killing* him. How often do we ourselves engage in accusations and petty revenge we know to be wrong, eating the "fruit of the tree" of distraction like our first parents, Adam and Eve?

And by acting from willful blindness and projections, they went on to experience the consequences of those actions, realizing their deepest fear: the Romans, the fall of Rome; and the Jews, the destruction of the Temple. Like them, we experience the built-in accountability and wrath for sin through our consequences, blaming God and others and ourselves, while having no idea why we're still sinning because we will not look at our projections, the snake in the garden with us.

Projections tend to greatly increase our inclination to distractions of sin and self-medication. Of course, when we are compelled by dark emotional and psychological forces that we do not understand or even "see"—often because we were wounded at early stages of development—we are truly less morally culpable. So, God sent his only Son to die out of mercy for us and our lack of self-awareness so that we could "see" and be healed.

Our deepest, oldest projections are so much a dark side of our personality that if he were to pull them out at the root, or too soon or all at once, the human psyche would shatter. They lie under our wounds and motivate all our worst sins and evils. And so, patiently and gently—while we beg him to "remove the sin from me!" over and over—he illuminates our wounds and their full contents through our pop quizzes—heart, soul, mind, and strength—in order to heal them completely, at the root. Our personality and its shadow are not removed at all, but are renewed and remain in tension, crucified with Christ, until we die: truth on the right, darkness on the left; heaven above, and earth below.

There is no way to order projections properly if we do not "see" the shadow or the snake, since, in one writer's secular view, "the snake in the Garden represents knowledge. That is why we fear knowledge of the truth, in this case, of the shadow."[16] We simply persist in projections and self-medication without questioning or knowing why. This illumination of our projections must be one of the greatest possible acts of love after Jesus's sacrifice, so that we don't continue to hate and kill ourselves and each other.

The Samaritan woman needed a personal relationship with Jesus and a proper way to express it in worship, one that would enable the tangible relationship of love to continue after he ascended to heaven and was physically gone. And so she opened her wounds and their judgments to Jesus and received his love in those darkest, lowest places.

The Pharisees are examples of what happens when we project anger onto God and do not open ourselves to the Lord in this way. Although they had proper worship (orthodoxy) up to the point at which Jesus revealed himself, they remained persistently stuck in legalistic, petty, superficial, judgmental interpretations of the law that lacked self-awareness. They even rejected Jesus's healing miracles, telling themselves that God would never be so outrageously merciful, that his power came from a malevolent source. That this Man is an impostor! (See Mark 8:11–13, Luke 6:6–11, Mt 21:24–27.)

They were murderous, hateful bullies—completely blind and ignorant of the fact that they were being manipulated by the evil one (just as we often are). Why were their judgments so persistent despite the God they outwardly worshiped speaking to them face-to-face through his Son? Jesus told the Pharisees they were "of your father the devil" and "not of God" (Jn 8:37–47), because the spirit of accusation, lies, and murder had taken hold in their souls. How can this be?

Exorcists tell us that demons attach themselves to our wounds[17] and attack us at this weakest point. There is a difference in the emotion of anger and the *spirit* of anger, a difference in a contemptuous accusation and the *spirit* of accusation. The presence of a corresponding spirit in our deepest heart wound is why such deep attitudes and behaviors almost always persist in defeating us even after years of therapy and a measure of emotional healing. They require the graces of deliverance, renunciation and repentance (turning away), and love in the soul.[18]

On the other hand, deliverance prayers alone do not usually offer permanent peace for the soul unless we also ask for and receive graces for healing the heart and mind, because despite the deliverance prayers, we continue projecting and cooperating with the enemy's accusations and lies in our wounds. Therefore, Jung said the genuine moral effort of Christian faith is more powerful than psychotherapy, though both are unwavering in their commitment to truth. Even Jung understood that psychotherapy is necessarily limited. Humans aren't simply a psyche or emotional and intellectual beings; we have a will and require love in the place we worship—the soul—or else we simply worship ourselves and our judgments with our wills unto destruction and hell.

Therefore, judgments are valuable in showing us whom we worship. They can reveal the truth of self-knowledge in our projections: I accuse my neighbor and even God because I accuse and judge myself. Where am I guilty of the same fault, or secretly wish I could be with immunity? Who is the real judge—and if God has not condemned me, who am I to condemn myself? Similarly, if I do not condemn myself, how can I condemn my neighbor? Rather, I want to love God for revealing myself and my neighbor to me and for freeing us both from my condemnation into love.

I reiterate that judgments are not simply observations, evaluations, or accountability. Boundaries are necessary for peace and healing. We are called to order and meaning by the Logos, and having been made in the image and likeness of God, we are made for establishing a measure of hierarchy and meaning through observation and evaluation and naming.

But judgments don't order. Judgments are loaded with cynicism, sarcasm, contempt, and disgust. They condemn. They separate. Ultimately, they turn us away from God.

Therefore, if they remain dark and unseen, accusations become the enemy in action in our souls and a major block to healing. They turn us not only away from others but ultimately away from God. We make vows and build walls against what we would otherwise experience from God through others by turning away from and labeling them and what they do as "bad" rather than seeing ourselves in them. We avoid erecting healthy boundaries for them and ourselves out of fear and therefore refuse to love. We abhor ourselves and "them" in divisions that prevent communion that evangelizes others into healing love.

The Samaritan woman accepted Jesus's illumination of her projections and errors in worship and went on to evangelize her fellow Samaritans. The Pharisees did not. Ultimately, the walls we set against God's Word are what determine our healing. He will not exceed the limits of our free will. We must invite him into our judgments so he can illumine them and pour his merciful love into them, so that we order properly, *with* him. As John Paul the Great pointed out, "The gracious way in which Jesus deals with the woman . . . is a model, helping others to be truthful without suffering in the challenging process of self-recognition."[19]

You will judge your wounder in a pop quiz, and you will judge yourself for actions and behaviors that proceed from that wound. Perhaps you will even judge God for allowing it. Ask for the grace to emotionally detach from the judgment in order to simply observe it, because judgments are *full* of information if we will stop judging ourselves for judging. When it comes to judging, we STOP. Let's review, and then we'll practice.

Let's Review

- Worship is my outward demonstration of love for God.
- God prescribes proper worship because it draws me into the closest possible love relationship with him and into communion with heavenly love.
- Jesus touches and heals me, now, through sacramental worship. Sacramental worship makes Jesus's healing love ritually and fully present to me.
- Authentic worship includes allowing him to illuminate and heal my judgments.
- Judgments are accusations against others and are projections I should probe for self-knowledge with the Holy Spirit. I worship myself when I judge myself and others.
- I discern my judgments by cooperating with him in the pop quizzes he allows by using the STOP Tool.
- In the T step of the STOP Tool, I love God with all my *heart* by expressing everything in my heart regarding my pop quizzes, identifying the main *emotion* in the pop quiz and the *memory* or memories associated with that emotion.
- In the T step of the STOP Tool, I love God with all my *soul* by worshiping properly: by asking God to illuminate the *judgments* in my pop quizzes and pour his forgiveness and mercy into them by helping me *forgive* myself and my wounder.

Invitation

I have often shared in my work that my husband has the "gift of criticism." He's a perfect quality control guy, because he spots imperfections immediately and is happy to share them. Like Moses, he has the gift of justice, but sometimes it leads to wrath and self-righteous judgments. I know, now, his gift of justice is a strength that can get out of balance as a shadow part of his personality, so that asking him to "stop it!" would be like asking an elephant to be a fish. Complicating matters, my father wound made me overly sensitive to his judgments, sometimes bitten out in criticism against me, and they deepened the sense that nothing I did was ever right. Therefore, I often overreacted in response.

My shadow is rebellion; the good side of that is an ability to take big risks. But the shadow emerges when I sense any vestige of manipulation or control with my super-sized, super-sensitive tyranny antennae; I go into full-blown resistance.

I was often punished and "on restriction," in my father's vernacular, for weeks at a time for infractions against rules that were sometimes clear and sometimes unspoken and arbitrary. In some cases what was deemed wrong was simply disliked, and I didn't always know I had done something wrong until I was punished. Restriction meant everything was removed from my bedroom except for furniture, books, and clothes. My radio, games, toys, posters, and pictures—even my musical jewelry box with the little ballerina on it—everything remotely fun was taken away, and I was required to sit on my bed in isolation and read or do schoolwork. If my schoolwork was complete, my father kept a ready supply of supplemental math workbooks for me to do. No play allowed. And weeks of isolation and silent treatment.

My husband and I, out of our wounds, have spent a lot of our marriage offering pop quizzes to one another and negotiating boundaries. We often disagreed about what constituted too much "play." I work long and hard; when I finish a project or a speaking event, I like to relax with streaming video or wine and friends, unwinding and eating and laughing. After all, as the famous line from the 1980s horror film *The Shining* says, "All work and no play makes Jack a dull boy."

My husband worked long and hard hours in a tense job and often felt others were lazy and did not have good work ethic. His criticism insulted me when I or anyone else played too much or too long. I am naturally conscientious and orderly (more so than he, according to testing);[20] he had nothing to do directly with my flourishing work, and I felt his criticism subtly marginalized it. Meanwhile, I had a lively relationship with God and didn't need or want him "helping" the Holy Spirit to make me see it his way. I felt his criticism was rooted in irrational fears from mother wounds and that he was restricting me. When he got judgmental, I faced the contradiction of wanting and needing to be humble and godly yet feeling irresistibly compelled to overdo the very things he hated, sometimes overtly, sometimes sneakily. I often saw my rebellion as a middle finger to tyranny.

In one of my pop quizzes with him, I was in the full emotional throes, nursing my judgment that he was too judgmental. He needed to learn mercy. He condemned viciously. I wasn't doing anything wrong. I was disgusted with his disgust. Because I felt his criticism and condemnation were unjustified, I felt justified in my own.

But I also had a lot of experience with my wounds through pop quizzes and the useful self-knowledge in them for healing. So I ran through the STOP Tool, based on Psalm 4:4–5 (RSV2CE): "Be angry, but sin not; commune with your own hearts on your beds, and be silent. Offer right sacrifices, and put your trust in the Lord."

S—Sin not;
T—Tell God everything in your heart, soul, mind, and strength;
O—Offer the right sacrifice;
P—Put your trust in God.

On the S step, I refrained from responding in anger, passively or aggressively, or criticizing him for his criticism. Remember that the T step is a reference to the *Shema:* "You shall love the Lord your God with all your heart, with all your soul, with all your mind, and with all your strength" (Mk 12:29–30). So I opened my heart, soul, mind, and strength to God's love: The anger in my *heart* was obvious; the feeling of badness (shame) in his condemnation was, too, because I had experienced it many times from my husband, and it was a familiar feeling in many memories with my father.

In the *soul* part of the T step, we examine the judgments we make against the wounder in our pop quizzes as projections of our own faults and inferiorities. Judgments contain contempt, disgust, accusation, cynicism, and condemnation. We shouldn't judge ourselves for judging; just notice the judgment.

I asked the Lord: *What is the judgment I am making about my husband in this immediate pop quiz, and what is the judgment I made about my father in the memories attached to these feelings of badness? How are these judgments a projection of my own vices or deficiencies?*

My judgments were clear: *He is too demanding and critical! He won't let me play!* But the projection was that *I* felt guilty for playing, partly because my father restricted play and therefore play felt irresponsible, partly because I sometimes overplayed and partly because my husband didn't like it, and I wanted to please him. I discovered a contradiction: I wanted to play because it is necessary and good, and everyone needs rest and leisure, but I wanted to overplay as a rebellion against his restrictions, and overplay is unnecessary and can even be sinful.

I allowed the judgment and contradiction into my awareness and talked to God about it. Was my play sinful? Sometimes. It certainly wasn't when I was a child. In this case? Yes. Definitely my husband didn't like it and was being overbearing about it. But I felt rebellious and judged myself for playing, because I was trained early that restrictions on playing were punishment, and

I did not want to be punished, so I overplayed. Then I judged myself for it, knowing that rebellion and lack of temperance are sins.

This is a recurring constellation of wound, emotion, and memories for me. Rebellion under perceived tyranny from men whom I love and respect (such as my husband) is my "one wound to rule them all," and criticism often felt shameful, particularly if I actually sinned. My husband's judgment against me provoked my rebellion because it was hypocritical: his wrath was intemperate, but he could not see it because he was blind in his judgment against me, while my sin was clear, acknowledged, confessed to him and God, and forgiven by God. Because the constellation of wound, emotion, and memories was familiar, I needed to detach myself from the wound, coach myself in love and truth, and walk in that knowledge: I need to play without self-judgment; play is not bad, but I must practice temperance. When I do not practice temperance, I must not judge myself but get up and do better next time. I forgave my husband for judging; I forgave myself for lack of temperance and judging. I had already forgiven my father for harsh, restrictive parenting.

I'll come back to this pop quiz in the next chapters for the mind and strength parts of the T step. For now, since I had loved God with all my heart and soul, I proceeded to the O step of the STOP Tool: I determined to allow my husband to overreact in judgment against me without retaliating and without judging him for his lack of temperance. I determined to allow myself a fall without judging myself. I determined to allow my husband to be angry and let the Holy Spirit deal with him. I determined to begin again in practicing temperance.

Can you see how judgments blind us from experiencing and learning from one another? A conflict arose, we judged one another, and we could not draw close in communion and love. When I worked through the judgments in my pop quiz, I could see I was projecting onto my husband my own judgment of myself for a fall. Was lack of temperance good? No, and I must take responsibility for self-control and depend on the Holy Spirit's help in moments of temptation to rebel and overplay. But my judgment revealed my own learned, irrational demands for perfection of myself at all times.

I was not allowed to make mistakes as a child. I was forced to obey sometimes unreasonable or uncommunicated demands, immediately, and when I did not, wrath, tyranny, and manipulation followed. I struggled with OCD, perfectionism, scruples, and depression anytime I did not live up to the picture of Christian perfectionism others articulated or I created in my mind. There was a time I judged God as controlling, of disallowing mistakes, of requiring immediate obedience, and punishing unknown infractions severely and harshly with suffering or pain. I judged my husband similarly when he criticized me. But I projected those judgments.

When I understood "there is therefore now no condemnation for those who are in Christ" (Rom 8:1) and that God judges neither me *nor* my husband for mistakes, I stopped demanding perfection from myself and stopped demanding it from my husband. I allowed him to criticize and God to work, and he became less critical. When my husband afforded me similar grace and mercy, I began to trust in his love and, therefore, trust in God's love. This is how releasing our judgments can lead to proper charity for ourselves and others, and communion and love with them. I submit that this is why God allows them, as Jesus taught. We see the speck in our brother's eye *because* there is a beam in our own. If we can ask the Holy Spirit to show us the beam in our eye, we can see both ourselves and our brother clearly. Ready to try it?

Benediction—LOVE the Word®

L | Listen (Receive the Word.)

Psalm 4:4–5 (RSV2CE): "Be angry, but sin not; commune with your own hearts on your beds, and be silent. Offer right sacrifices, and put your trust in the LORD."

S—Sin not;
T—Tell God everything in your heart, soul, mind, and strength;
O—Offer the right sacrifice;
P—Put your trust in God.

O | Observe (Observe your relationships and circumstances.)

With the Holy Spirit and in his presence, think back to your latest pop quiz. Try to place yourself back into the situation, remembering with all your senses.[21] Without judgment, observe whether or not you sinned and, if you did, how (S). Remembering that the T step is a reference to the *Shema*, tell God everything in your heart and soul, the two parts we've covered so far.

Heart: *What is the main emotion I am feeling or felt? What is the memory behind this emotion and the symptoms I'm experiencing? When is the first time I can remember feeling exactly this way?* Try to stay here until a memory surfaces, asking the Holy Spirit to reveal it.

Soul: *What do I feel in my heart about the person in my immediate pop quiz and the person in my wounded memory who hurt me? What is the accusation or judgment I made or am making about these people? How is this judgment a projection of my own fault or inferiority or a desire to do the same or similar with immunity?*

Completing the *heart* part of the *Shema* involves *emotions and memories*; the *soul* part involves *judgments and forgiveness*. Remembering that forgiveness is the cancellation of a debt, forgive your wounders: *In the Name of Jesus, I forgive _____ for _____*. Remember to forgive yourself, too. Perhaps you'd like to visualize bringing your wounder(s) to the foot of the Cross and leaving them there with Jesus and Our Lady.

When we have completed the S and T steps, we are ready to "offer the right sacrifice" (O). Ask: *Holy Spirit, what is the right thing to do in this situation now?* Then (P) "put your trust in him" for every outcome. Take your time and wait on the Holy Spirit through each step, remembering that the STOP Tool will get easier, and then become automatic, because you'll have a wealth of opportunities to practice in plenty more pop quizzes. If you do not receive a "right sacrifice," do nothing as a sacrifice unless or until you do.

V | Verbalize (Pray through your thoughts and emotions.)

Repeat back to him everything you believe he said or revealed. You may want to write your reflections in a journal.[22]

Lord, this STOP Tool made me realize . . .
I had difficulty with . . .
I am afraid of . . .
I need help with . . .

E | Entrust (May it be done to me according to your Word.)

In your Name, Lord Jesus, Son of the living God, I ask you to heal every emotion and judgment associated with this memory, and heal this wound in my soul. Jesus, I ask you to help me to forgive myself and the other person(s) completely. I receive your healing love. Amen.

Four

With All Your Mind

Jesus Heals Deafness... and Transforms Toxic Thinking

> Then he returned from the region of Tyre, and went through Sidon to the Sea of Galilee, through the region of the Decap'olis. And they brought to him a man who was deaf and had an impediment in his speech; and they besought him to lay his hand upon him. (Mk 7:31–32)

In his chest, he feels a low rumble of air vibrating in the village as he pushes through knots of people to get home for the evening meal, his hands full of figs. Two men gesture wildly at him, and with revulsion, he spots a crumb of evening bread caught in one of the men's beards. *Why everyone so excited?*

His face pinched with exhaustion, his eyes squint like a mole's as he concentrates on reading their lips, but the low light of dusk makes the effort to understand their words and body language futile. He smells strong body odor and spits on the ground in disgust when one of the men he knows from synagogue tries to drag him forward. He can't sign "NO!" because of the figs he holds in both hands, so he tosses his head and pulls away.

Not rude! Not stupid! $&%# idiots!* The sound is guttural and intelligible, he knows, so he screams it again into the silence, resisting the impulse to grunt for the speaker to repeat himself for a third time. He *wants* to understand;

he just.

can't.

hear.

He's missing large chunks of whatever is happening that's gotten everyone so worked up. Surrounded by constant silence. Alone with dark thoughts. Continual misunderstandings and invisibility mark his daily existence on the fringes of everyday celebrations and group conversations. His depression is a tunic as dark as third watch, hanging heavier than the heat. *Why no one try communicate clear?*

Turning on his heel, he feels his heart sucking down into the weight of deep isolation and lies that have shaped his identity his entire deaf life: "Rude. Stupid. Not deaf; you not *listen!*" He smashes into someone standing too close and drops the pile of figs, cursing vilely at him, the figs, his life, everyone.

They both step to the side and squat, their backs and bodies low to the ground. This nuisance person reaches out, but he doesn't touch the figs. The deaf man looks up and gasps at something striking that glints from the other man's pupils, thinking to himself, *He try touch me?* The intimacy is so uncomfortable he almost pulls away, but the plaintive light in the other man's eyes seems tightly *personal*, so he leans forward instinctively, trying to catch any nuance in communication from this unknown stranger.

But Jesus doesn't speak; it's too dark for lip-reading. Instead he sticks two skinny fingers right into the deaf man's ear holes, which would have been supremely uncomfortable except it happened so fast. There is a loud whooshing sound that makes the deaf man dizzy. With one hand, Jesus steadies him, and the whooshing sound settles, too. He watches with incredulity as Jesus spits on a finger of his other hand and reaches out toward the man's mouth; it opens on its own. Then, God help him, in the whooshing sound he *hears* a deep guttural groan that he thinks at first is his own, and then a Word,

"*Ephphatha.*" Be opened.

God's Word Makes Us Hear

Why are we so deaf to the truth of love? Because we do not know and believe God's Word.

In commenting on this healing, the church fathers say that listening to and speaking evil makes one deaf and mute; a deaf person cannot hear the Words of God or open his mouth to speak them. But let us not assume "evil" is merely some form of malice or occult practice, although they're certainly evil. Rather, Jesus told the Pharisees in John 8 that their root evil was lies, and that the "father of lies" had captured their minds. Throughout the Old and New Testaments, we learn that "evil" is ultimately a "heart of unbelief."[1] As long as we cannot or will not, whether out of ignorance or laziness, hear or speak God's Word of truth into our lives and live from it in faith, we remain tyrannized by lies and a lack of belief in God's all-consuming love.

The lies we come to believe about ourselves often take root early in our development. "The purification of our hearts has to do with paternal and maternal images" (*CCC*, 2779). *It is these accusations that we probe with the Holy Spirit in the "mind" part of our pop quizzes:* "Love the Lord your God with all your heart, and with all your soul, and with all your mind . . ." (Mk 12:30). Satan is called the accuser of the brethren who accuses them day and night (Rv 12:10). Accusations and lies are the enemy's primary tool against us. When we listen to his accusations and lies, we live in agreement with him. God forbid!

My earliest wounded memories involve being "in trouble" with my father. When I was around four, I was fascinated with his blue dandruff shampoo and poured a whole bottle into the bathtub to look at the pretty blue swirls it made against the white ceramic. As punishment, he drew a chalk circle on my bedroom door a couple of inches taller than I was, so that I had to stand on tiptoe to reach it when he pushed my nose into it and made me stand there for hours under watchful intimidation. The next day, I ate the entire piece of chalk in a silent act of rebellion. Even now, I know what a veneer bedroom door in military-assigned housing smells like. That event—one of my earliest memories—was the beginning of a "badness" lie that fueled a lifetime of rebellious tendencies against control, and the badness lie only seemed to be reinforced every time I felt "in trouble": "You are bad."

Perhaps you suffered as a child. Maybe you've wondered why God allows suffering, particularly in children, when their personalities and temperaments are only just being formed. In his apostolic letter *Salvifici Doloris* (*Redemptive Suffering*), St. John Paul II said, "To suffer means to become particularly susceptible, particularly open to the working of the salvific powers of God. God has confirmed his desire to act especially through suffering."

Perhaps we should make an important distinction: He doesn't make us suffer so he can work through it; we suffer because of the Fall, and he redeems it. When God places children under adult authority by natural law, adults become responsible for them—nurturing them, protecting them, teaching them, and disciplining them. When we embrace that responsibility as adults, as parents and collectively, children flourish and come to a fuller understanding of who God is and what he desires from us. When we don't live up to that responsibility, as parents and collectively, the consequences are dire: children suffer.

> Whoever causes one of these little ones who believe in me to sin, it would be better for him to have a great millstone fastened round his neck and to be drowned in the depth of the sea. (Mt 18:6)

Where were the adults when you suffered? Why blame God when the adults in authority . . . weren't? By returning to those memories, we are not assigning blame, anyway, but recalling our earliest impressions and beliefs about ourselves in order to ask the Holy Spirit to reveal self-knowledge in our projections.

Although we may have suffered as children, perhaps it can teach us to hear God. That seems to be Jesus's model: "Although he was a Son, he learned obedience through what he suffered" (Heb 5:8). The word *obedience* means "to hear," and the picture is that of leaning forward to catch even the whisper of what is said. Although suffering seems to obscure the goodness of God,[2] maybe it's also the key to loving him and being loved by him, particularly with all our mind. Because it can motivate us, in our painful adult confusion over the goodness of God for what he allows, to lean in and hear his voice in it, to get his perspective. Our leaning into his Word allows him to pour his love into our suffering, and heal it. He does this with truth. Truth combats the negativity and lies that make us deaf to love. The truth of God's Word provides boundaries that keep in what is nurturing and keep out what is destructive.

Paradise, a Walled Garden

Recently, I attended Jordan Peterson's We Who Wrestle with God tour in Nashville. One of the ideas he presented was the idea of a walled garden in Genesis. I dug into his premise, and indeed, *paradise* means *para* ("around") and *disus* ("wall"). The Hebrew word for *garden* in Genesis means "fenced" or "walled."

I've been thinking about that a lot in light of Matthew 18 and the necessity of boundaries that keep in what is nurturing and keep out what is destructive from the "gardens" of our hearts, families, etc. Wasn't it God's command, his Word, that "walled off" the trees of life and knowledge of good and evil? Isn't his revelation of truth the only way we even know what is dangerous to us and what preserves and promotes life and love?

The term "law" has gotten a bad rap in our day, such that it has come to connote arbitrary, suffocating rules. But the Hebrew people saw God's Law as a gift, a personal revelation of God to them that provided bumpers or guardrails to enable them to move safely, skillfully, fruitfully, and peacefully along the road of life. I'd say we need to recover the safety of the "law" today, wouldn't you?

When we don't know God's truth, we persist in the lies that we have come to believe about ourselves in hurts, offenses, and suffering. These lies are often instilled very early, even with loving parents, because our parents, too, have lived from deficits of love. When we persist in those lies, we live in agreement with the enemy, the "father of lies." When we live in agreement with the enemy, our inner garden is open to his ransacking, destruction, and chaos: "My people are destroyed for lack of knowledge" (Hos 4:6).

Pop quizzes are the Holy Spirit's way of leading us to healing. Until we begin cooperating with them, the lies we have come to believe about ourselves, God, and our neighbors continue to deepen and solidify, and we live in purposelessness and futility from that negativity (Heb 3:7–19). As those toxic lies take root, nest, and multiply in seasons of deprivation and neediness, we become "deaf" to truth. Only putting on "the mind of Christ" (1 Cor 2:16) by *believing* (walking in) the truth of the sacraments and scripture will unstop our ears and make us attuned to the voice of God in our lives.

A Nest of Cockroaches

Remember when speaking on healing the heart, I compared emotions to puppies in how we need to treat them gently and give them boundaries? Well, lies and other negative thoughts are a different animal.

We do not tolerate lies and negative thoughts. Ever. Always eliminate them as soon as you recognize them. They're like cockroaches: resilient, fast-breeding, and carriers of spiritual bacteria and disease. Therefore, we do not allow a single negative, lying cockroach into the safety and warmth of our mind's walled "garden."

Interestingly, the cockroach's scientific name, *Blattodea*, tells us the strategy we should use for lies and negativity. Derived from the Latin *blatta*, it means an insect that "shuns the light."[3] We prevent lies and negativity from nesting in our minds with the light of God's Word. We speak it audibly. We remind and coach ourselves in the truth of God's Word until we have finally heard it in our hearts and "seen" it with our spiritual eye.

Neuroscience has demonstrated that emotions are attached to thoughts,[4] so that changing our thoughts will change our emotions. Biologically speaking, information comes into the brain through the five senses. The information is evaluated through current knowledge and previous experience as safe or dangerous. If the experience is evaluated as dangerous, the emotion of fear erupts in order to get us moving in fight-or-flight. We feel this fear in our bodies, where our hearts beat rapidly with adrenaline, our breathing may become shallow, and our thinking becomes foggy. We're not supposed to be thinking, after all, but running or defending ourselves, so strategizing next steps becomes difficult as instinct takes over.

St. Thomas Aquinas said that the purpose of emotion is to assist us in executing proper action.[5] But emotions are fickle, and not always an accurate indicator of reality. For instance, a movie may scare us or make us cry, but it's not real; it's a movie. If a perceived danger is based on emotion, if the brain recognizes past trauma in a current situation rather than actual physical danger, we may experience what psychologist Dr. Daniel Goleman called an amygdala hijack,[6] in which the fight-or-flight stress response kicks in unnecessarily. It's at this point that we can make important choices and adjustments to our thinking.

To regain control, practice STOP. If we persistently counter the fear-lie with truth, the fear subsides. But if we do not challenge negative, fearful thoughts, if we ruminate on them and allow those cockroaches to breed, in about twenty-four hours they become a permanent part of our physiology.

In her book *Who Switched Off My Brain?* Dr. Caroline Leaf explains that there are only two emotions, fear and love; the rest proceed from these. The Bible agrees: "There is no fear in love, but perfect love casts out fear" (1 Jn 4:18). "Perfect" means mature. It takes practice to learn to replace lies with truth, fear with love, cockroaches with light; it takes time to consistently mature in authentic love. That's what this book and our whole lives in the university of love are about. So, we cannot get in a hurry with ourselves and others.

Filling in and rerouting old mind ruts takes time and determination as we hear and practice God's Word. On the other hand, research in neuroscience shows that toxic, negative lies and emotions are predicable, controllable, transformable, and healable, even after long-term habits of painful fear and negativity. There's an entire modality in psychotherapy called Cognitive Behavioral Therapy that's devoted to changing one's negative, irrational thinking. But God's Word is the best modality, because it alone has the inherent power to produce an effect: "So shall my word be that goes forth from my mouth; it shall not return to me empty, but it shall accomplish that which I purpose, and prosper in the thing for which I sent it" (Is 55:11); and "the word of God is living and active, sharper than any two-edged sword, piercing to the division of soul and spirit, of joints and marrow, and discerning the thoughts and intentions of the heart" (Heb 4:12).

Think about it: Can you discern between your own soul and spirit or thoughts and intentions? I can't. Cognitive Behavioral Therapy can't. But God's Word can and does. God's Word heals "deafness" to truth, and it *heals* our minds in love as we employ it against the lies and negativity in our lives.

Lies and negativity begin and nest in the mind; therefore, they must be stopped in the mind. And to do that, we must know

God's Word. When we do not have a steady diet of scripture, we do not have the truth we need to combat the lies and accusations we have come to believe about ourselves in our suffering.

Interestingly, the sword of truth—the Word of God—is the only offensive weapon mentioned in scripture (Eph 6:10–18); we have no power to overcome the enemy on our own. Knowing truth is so important that much of my work with people in the Love Heals Masterclass and consultations[7] is in this area, because God's people "are destroyed for lack of knowledge" (Hos 4:6).

Willful Deafness?

The word *destroyed* means to perish or be cut off, to be unable to speak and hear as in deafness. These things occur not because God has neglected to speak the truth in his Word, nor because he strikes us deaf in retaliation for our disobedience. Rather, it's because we have *chosen* not to know, believe, or hear it and have therefore been cut off in continued silence. Willful deafness to truth leads inevitably to destruction.

For example, I worked for over a year with a surgeon who had been physically disabled with a mysterious fatigue combined with a stomach issue for almost a decade. The Mayo Clinic, Johns Hopkins, and a number of other top-notch hospitals and doctors found no organic cause and had no explanation for his debilitation. He got in touch with me after hearing me speak at an event, and we began working on his pop quizzes. Predictably, a pattern emerged: for the course of his entire life, he had said yes when he meant no. Partly, this habit was due to his sensitive, gentle personality and agreeable temperament, but ultimately, it was because the view of God that he learned growing up, both from the Church and his parents, was vengeful, condemning, and, to use his phrase, "OFMAYF—one false move and you're ———."

If he enjoyed something, he denied himself doing it as a sacrifice; if someone wanted something from him that he did not really want to do, he did it anyway because, to him, charity always meant that one must do for others to the exclusion of oneself. He felt God was punishing him with his sickness for having fun or some unknown infraction, but I knew his body was stepping in to help him because he had lived inauthentically his entire life and was projecting this angry, accusatory view of himself onto God.

Predictably, he was full of resentment. He all but hated himself for his habit of saying yes when he meant no, and he judged friends as stupid for not knowing he did not really like them and never had. We discovered the pop quiz trigger for his illness was saying yes to something he did not want to do or saying no to something he did want to do: he would become sick and unable to get out of bed in order to be excused from commitments he had dishonestly made, in a way that helped him feel guilt-free; or he would become too sick to enjoy himself, because, in his mind, that was not allowed.

This highly intelligent man was locked in illness-producing lies and emotions, but he learned to identify the root emotion associated with the onset of his sickness; he learned to let his yes be yes and his no be no, and to reject the enemy's lie ("I am bad and am being punished") as having no basis in biblical truth or reality. He began speaking truth into his life and living from it, recognizing the projection of his false judgments about God and how God felt about him. He realized that his sickness was his body's way of protecting him from things he did not want to do but had committed to out of fear of displeasing others and, therefore, God. He forgave himself for having succumbed for decades to these horrible, self-defeating lies. As he consistently and thoroughly worked through his pop quizzes with me, his health was completely restored. A miracle healing! Slow, but sure.

What provoked his greatest fears, the ones that drove all the dysfunction in his heart, soul, mind, and strength? Neediness and deprivation.

So You're Needy?

Human relationships and other substitutes are too limited to satisfy your emotional needs—you know this, right? Does the depth of your neediness scare you to death? Have you ever really allowed yourself to *feel* it? Does neediness and weakness in yourself and others disgust you? Do you judge yourself for neediness and project that condemnation onto others?

Welcome to the human race.

You were created to need—to need other people and, ultimately, to need God. Remember that love has been irrefutably proven to be the most important human need. In fact, you were created with an abyss of need meant to be infinitely satisfied with an infinite love. You were created to be cherished that deeply. Therefore, lack of love, deprivation of love, is our greatest suffering.

Suffering is inseparable from man's earthly existence, as attested to by St. John Paul II in his apostolic letter, *Salvifici Doloris* (*Redemptive Suffering*). Although we share suffering and death with the animal world, only humans *know* they will die. Only humans suffer and ask *why*, as St. John Paul II noted in the same letter. God expects that question, and he has answered definitively through the Son. "Suffering seems to belong to man's transcendence: it is one of those points in which man is in a certain sense 'destined' to go beyond himself, and he is called to this in a mysterious way. . . . Love is also the fullest source of the answer to the question of the meaning of suffering."

Deprivation wounds.

Love heals.

The level of shame and guilt and disgust we feel due to the neediness we feel and find in ourselves and others requires that we recognize that it's part of the human condition. Adam and Eve were created needy: they needed food, water, work, and intimate relationship *before* sin ever entered the Garden. So neediness is not a matter of sinfulness, but createdness.

The tragedy of sin was the alienation of Adam and Eve from God as Source: of love, of provision, of emotional safety. They could no longer be needy with one another or God without self-consciousness and condemnation. Healing, then, involves restoring our connection to God as our source of love, provision, and emotional safety. We work not only toward dependency on him but also away from self-sufficiency. So embrace your neediness, direct it properly to God, and you will grow out of leeching and stoic behaviors that prevent you from fully satiating the neediness that otherwise eats you alive.

Neediness exposes our weakness, vulnerability, and inability to love and be loved. And what follows is the enemy's lie that we (or our neighbor) are unworthy of love. We love God with all our minds by directing our neediness to him and combating lies that block the flow of healing love between us and God and us and our neighbor. In Jesus's encounter with the blind man, the Samaritan woman, and the deaf man—all who were deemed unworthy—Jesus initiates healing by directing human neediness to himself.

Interestingly, there have been many "core wounds" iterated throughout healing circles in the Church, such as abandonment, confusion, fear, hopelessness, powerlessness, rejection, and shame. To be sure, those are all lies and accusations of the enemy leveled against every Christian and projected onto us and by us. But in my experience, they all boil down to "the one wound that rules them all": worthlessness. Perhaps the root of all accusations against humanity is worthlessness. I say that because it's the only wound associated with a proper name in scripture.

Love Blocker: Worthlessness

Growing up, it seemed to me that my dad was always in a state of no-contact silent treatment with somebody or other in his family. So when his brother died, my sister and I saw relatives at his funeral we had seen only a few times our entire lives.

Given our family history, I dreaded what was in store: a reunion initially presented as "bridge building" degenerating into more painful drama.

That night, in a private discussion with my father, he related his regret for demanding that I push my wedding date out and refusing to come at all or speak to me in the years since. I was already weary from the funeral, so I recall little detail of our conversation except that I was deeply and pleasantly surprised by the uncharacteristic olive branch. Grasping my hands warmly between his and leaning in so close I could smell the breath mint over his familiar cologne, he told me he had been so adamant, then, about my waiting to marry because he knew I could have been somebody and he felt I was wasting my potential. For my part, despite my young age, I had refused to push the date out because my not-yet husband and I were cohabitating, and I wanted to end that situation as soon as possible and stop living in sin.

After my talk with my father following the funeral, I remember returning home in a fog. I was irritable and snappish—depressed. I cried at every provocation. I was spoiling for a fight (no surprise) and picked one with my husband. For weeks I couldn't function normally, but I also couldn't discern why I was so emotional. I remember writing in my prayer journal, "Why do I feel so *worthless*?" and gouging deep holes in the tear-stained pages with my pen. Why was I so desperately sad?

Always faithful, he answered me *through his Word*.

Providentially, a friend and I were working through a Bible study on wellness; that week, we studied emotions as the voice of relationships. I couldn't have been more stunned by the words on the page if they had leaped up and slapped me: I was in the throes of an amygdala hijack, a "historical emotion" meltdown.

What Are Historical Emotions?

Psychology tells us historical emotions are those emotions that occurred earlier in life that are reexperienced later. A historical emotion has been felt repeatedly to the point that it takes up residence in the individual and lies dormant until she experiences events that reflect the earlier painful experience. At this point, the emotion is reactivated and reexperienced in a way that seems to bypass the will and conscience, moving someone from feeling calm to inexplicably frantic in a matter of milliseconds. She might feel blindsided and wonder, *Where did that come from?* or *What was that?* Trying to make sense out of the feeling from a present perspective ends in frustration, because the key is in the past.

In my mind, I groped for the onset of the darkness and realized it was the funeral—that conversation. *I could have been somebody,* my father had said.

But I wasn't.

Do you ever feel that way? "You could have been seen, if you'd been worth the time. You should have been loved, if you'd been worth the effort. You would have been cherished, if you weren't worthless."

While anxiety is an existence lie that usually proceeds from a mother wound, worthlessness is an identity lie that usually proceeds from a father wound. Worthlessness may be the most pernicious, pervasive, evil lie Satan tells each of us, and a hypocritical one as well. I reject that identity lie in the name of Jesus. Here's why.

Biblical names reveal something about the place or person named. At the same time as the insight into historical emotions, I was writing my own Bible study and discovered an interesting, rarely used biblical term that was a proper name in the context I was studying: "For what partnership have righteousness and iniquity? Or what fellowship has light with darkness? What accord has Christ with Be'lial? Or what has a believer in common with an unbeliever?" (2 Cor 6:14–15).

Notice, first, that the terms are presented in opposition to one another: righteousness disputes iniquity (meaning crookedness); light battles darkness; Christ opposes Belial; believers challenge unbelievers. There's no partnership, no fellowship, no oneness, nothing in common. These terms are complete opposites. What I found next stunned me.

I always look up biblical names to see what they reveal. Belial, it turned out, was an etymological revelation. The Greek is translated *Beliar* or *Belial*. From two common Hebrew words *beli* (without) and *ya'al* (value), this word is usually translated *worthless* throughout the Old Testament. But, later, it became used as a proper name for Satan (2 Cor 6:15).

Oh, what love gushed into my soul at the knowledge God did not find me worthless at all; in fact, he remains in eternal opposition to that lie! The Lord poured his love into my worthlessness wound with the truth of his Word, and I saw that Belial accuses us with his own name. What a hypocrite. What a liar!

The remedy for worthlessness is also offered in that passage. Remember that worthlessness is *the* identity lie—"the one wound to rule them all"—most often from a father wound. St. Paul goes on to quote a verse from a Messianic Servant Song with a line from the covenant God made with David in the Old Testament: he says "come out of" or separate from worthlessness—that it's "unclean"—and God will become a real Father to you.

Interestingly, the words *devil* and *unclean* are closely linked in the scriptures. Many of the deaf and mute that Jesus healed were said to be tormented by demons and possessed by devils. Were they possessed by worthlessness?

Hear the Word of the Lord!

Lies are from the enemy. Worthlessness is a devil with a proper name. Lies are unclean and multiply like cockroaches. Deafness to God's Word destroys you with lies and uncleanness, makes you mute and unable to speak of him and praise him as your heavenly Father.

Come out! *Ephphatha!*

Let's Review

- I love the Lord with all my heart, soul, mind, and strength by cooperating with him in the pop quizzes he allows and by using the STOP Tool.
- In the T step of the STOP Tool, I love God with all my *heart* by expressing everything in my heart regarding my pop quizzes, identifying the main *emotion* in the pop quiz and the *memory* or memories associated with that emotion, and allowing the Holy Spirit to pour his love into them.
- In the T step of the STOP Tool, I love God with all my *soul* by telling God all the *judgments* I find in my soul, forgiving myself and my wounder(s), and allowing the Holy Spirit to pour his *forgiveness* and mercy into them.
- Listening to, believing, and speaking lies makes me spiritually deaf and mute.
- The enemy exploits my neediness, woundedness, and deafness to God's Word with lies. Satan is the father of lies. Fear, lies, negativity, and accusations come from the enemy.
- I battle Satan's lies in my mind by hearing and speaking the truth of God's Word.
- I was created needy. Neediness is not a matter of sinfulness.
- God created me from love, sustains me in love, grows me in love, and will continually supply my need for love (Phil 4:19), because it is my most basic need.
- I get my love needs met by building an intimate love relationship with the Lord through his Word.
- The Bible says God is diametrically opposed to worthlessness, because worthlessness is a devil. The worthlessness identity lie is the "one wound to rule them all."
- I hear by knowing and applying God's Word to my life.
- In the T step of the STOP Tool, I love the Lord with all my *mind* by refuting *lies*, negativity, and fear of deprivation with the *truth* of God's Word and applying it to my life.

Invitation

If you get nothing else from this study, I pray you get this truth: you are loved. By virtue of your existence, you are worthy of love. You are worthy to be. More transparently than you can possibly endure, you are loved. "Hidden" is not the same as "absent." He hides himself *for* you, not *from* you. He withholds himself from smothering you and overwhelming you completely with the heart-exploding love we call "heaven," because to see yourself in him, all at once—all your projections, wounds, sins, pain, and lies—as transparently as he sees and loves you, would be beyond bearing.[8]

This is why healing is necessarily slow, precept upon precept, line upon line, here a little, there a little, faith to faith (Is 28:10 and Rom 1:17). We learn slowly, not because we are stupid, but because we are limited by sensory information that we can gather and process in increments of time. We do not have to frantically seek out the places in our hearts, souls, minds, and bodies that need mercy and healing. That's what pop quizzes are for. Wait on God. Allow him to show you, gently and slowly, where he is working to heal you.

His promise is healing in heart, soul, mind, and strength. The measure with which we trust him for, conform ourselves to, and open our hearts, souls, minds, and bodies to that healing love is the measure we receive that healing.

Worthlessness blocks healing because it is an identity lie, possibly the most vicious and prolific lie, because it is an attack against the inherent dignity of a person that issues from all being; it bears the stench of sulfur and all the fury of worthlessness itself. If I feel worthless, I will not seek his love and healing. Worthlessness is the lie Satan dares to tell each of us to exploit our shame and feelings of isolation from our own sin and from when we were sinned against, because he is worthlessness personified and he projects his own nothingness on all that is. Worthlessness is one of Satan's most prevailing, successful lies against God's children. Refuse to listen to that lie another day!

Because you're learning about pop quizzes with me, I bet you've had a new one recently. Surprise! Time to practice! Let's work through it to the point we've gotten in the STOP Tool so far, and start replacing those lies with truth.

Benediction—LOVE the Word®

L | Listen (Receive the Word.)

Psalm 4:4–5 (RSV2CE): "Be angry, but sin not; commune with your own hearts on your beds, and be silent. Offer right sacrifices, and put your trust in the LORD."

S—Sin not;
T—Tell God everything in your heart, soul, mind, and strength;
O—Offer the right sacrifice;
P—Put your trust in God.

O | Observe (Observe your relationships and circumstances.)

With the Holy Spirit and in his presence, think back to your latest pop quiz. Try to place yourself back into the situation, remembering everything about it[9] using all your senses. Without judgment, observe whether you sinned or not (S), and if you did, how. Remembering that the T step is a reference to the *Shema,* tell God everything in your heart, soul, and mind, the parts we've covered so far.

Heart: *What is the main emotion I am feeling or felt? What is the memory behind this emotion and the symptoms I'm experiencing? When is the first time I can remember feeling exactly this way?*

Stay here until a memory surfaces, asking the Holy Spirit to reveal it. When you have a memory or memories, move to the soul.

Soul: *What do I feel in my heart about the person in my immediate pop quiz and the person in my wounded memory who hurt me? What is the judgment I made or am making about these people? How is this judgment a projection of my own fault or inferiority, or a desire to do the same or similar with immunity?*

Remembering that forgiveness is the cancellation of a debt, forgive your wounders: *In the Name of Jesus, I forgive _____ for _____.* Remember to forgive yourself, too. Perhaps you'd like to visualize bringing your wounder(s) to the foot of the Cross and leaving them there.

Mind: *Holy Spirit, what is the lie or lies I came to believe about myself in this pop quiz and the memory attached? Holy Spirit, what is the truth you want to exchange with me for that lie?*[10]

Try not to analyze it or figure it out, just listen and receive, because the Holy Spirit often says things far differently than we could imagine. The most powerful, healing truth comes from God's Word. If you need help, thumb through the truths I compiled for you in the back of the Working through Pop Quizzes Workbook. When you have both the lie and the truth, renounce the lie(s) and announce the truth:

In the Name of Jesus, I renounce the lie that . . .
In the Name of Jesus, I announce the truth that . . .

Completing the *heart* part of the *Shema* concerns *emotions* and *memories*; the *soul* part includes *judgments* and *forgiveness*. The *mind* part involves replacing *lies* with *truth*.

When we have completed the S and T steps, we are ready to "offer the right sacrifice" (O). Ask: *Holy Spirit, what is the right thing to do in this situation now?*

Put your trust in God (P). Take your time and wait on the Holy Spirit through each step, remembering that the STOP Tool will get easier to practice, and then become automatic, because you'll have a wealth of opportunities to practice in plenty more pop quizzes.

V | Verbalize (Pray through your thoughts and emotions.)

Repeat back to him everything you believe he said or revealed. You may want to write your reflections in a journal.[11]

Lord, this STOP Tool made me realize . . .
I had difficulty with . . .
I am afraid of . . .
I need help with . . .

E | Entrust (May it be done to me according to your Word.)

In your Name, Lord Jesus, Son of the living God, I ask you to heal every emotion and judgment associated with this memory, and heal this wound in my soul. Jesus, I ask you to help me to forgive myself and this person or these people completely. I renounce the worthlessness lie. I announce the truth that I am blessed. I announce the truth that I am good. I announce the truth that I live and move and have my being in your love (Acts 17:28). I receive and rest in your healing love. Amen.

Five

With All Your Strength

Jesus Restores the Paralytic... and Heals Our Bodies

> As he was teaching, there were Pharisees and teachers of the law sitting by, who had come from every village of Galilee and Judea and from Jerusalem; and the power of the Lord was with him to heal. And behold, men were bringing on a bed a man who was paralyzed, and they sought to bring him in and lay him before Jesus. (Lk 5:17–18)

Everyone seems to think paralysis is contagious. Could imprisonment be any better a descriptor? Total lack of privacy. Cut off from almost all physical intimacy and near total deprivation of pleasure. Forced into accepting help, and feeling the need to justify it. He even misses cleaning up dishes after a meal.

He despises this total dependency that robs him of dignity until he feels something less than human. And he secretly resents those who help him; he feels like an unending burden even to the four who love him. But he also knows that if he doesn't ask for help, he's completely stranded and exposed. Unable to scratch the itch, take the walk, pour the sip, pee in privacy, cut the lamb, stretch in the sun; always depending on someone else to deliver his most basic needs. I mean, bowels. How can something so normal take so long and be so complicated?

At first he had hope. Then he realized nothing was going to change. Then he wished for death, to no longer be forced to live this way. It's pure hell. Extreme emotional dysregulation, outbursts of crying and anger. Completely numb to the world, living only in his mind. Existing in a shell, a limp, dead body.

He wants to be touched again, loved again. He wants to feel standing-up hugs. He wants to walk beside someone, holding hands by day and making love at night. He wants to pound out his anger, to dance and work the grain. He uses humor a lot in situations he can't control. But it's not funny. None of it. What bothers him most is uncontrollable neck spasms. Yet, none of that compares to *this* kind of powerlessness.

What he does have is determined friends. When one of them suggested they go see Jesus, it seemed crazy and even fun to him. He'd heard Jesus healed a blind man, a deaf man, a leper; he didn't believe it, even though the town was stirring—with fear, with hope, with jealousy—and it seemed the whole village had turned out in curiosity and desperation.

Nothing had prepared him for the terrifying suspense of what it would actually take to get him there, in front of the healer. If they drop him . . . He wonders how much worse it can get than paralysis, closing his eyes as the four of them lower him toward the ground. Truth be told, he doesn't really think the Jesus guy can help him. He had just been excited to get out of the stifling, lonely boredom of his pathetic life for a few minutes.

When they arrived at the house where Jesus was, and saw the crowds were too thick for him to get in, he told them to take him home. Instead his friends hatched up an insane plan B to get in from the top of the villa. Despite his vehement protests, they carried him up the steep steps to the roof, then pushed the stone roller to one side, away from the grain and fruit that was flattened and drying in the sun. Estimating where Jesus must have been standing, they pulled up some tiles and dug a hole to create an open space between the beams. Then, as people coughed and griped when rubble fell through the hole, the four friends started lowering him inside.

The distance between himself and his friends, now, sends him into panic; cold sweat prickles his neck. He feels faint as black spots form in his line of vision. His dead weight rolls dangerously close to the edge of the mat; it's a long way down to the stone floor below. "Help me!" he wants to shout. But no one can steady him; no one can reach; he's hanging between heaven and earth.

He can hear and smell the pack of people jammed in the room below, but turning his head as far to the right as possible, he can't see them. He sees the ropes in his friends' hands and the tops of their heads peeking through the ceiling as they strain to lower him slowly and carefully. He hears grunts of exertion, and feels a drop of salty sweat fall through the hole and land on his lip, but he can't wipe it.

He hits the floor with a thud. Everyone has stepped back to make room, peering up into the shaft of light as the dust and ropes fall, limp as his arms and legs. A rumble of indignation over the destruction of property begins to ripple, but fizzles out when Jesus looks up with something like respect. The four jubilant men are peering through the hole at the top, wiggling like children waiting for *ima*[1] to finish honey-cakes for Sabbath dessert. Yes, it suddenly feels like Sabbath: quiet, soft, slow, festive, peaceful.

"Man, your sins are forgiven you."

The paralytic does not know it was Jesus who spoke; both he and Jesus are looking intently at his friends through the hole in the roof, marveling at *their* determination, *their* anticipation, *their* faith, hope, and love. It's impossible not to see and feel. He feels desperately thankful for them, for all they've done for him over the years, and a weird flush of warmth descends on his head, over his face, down his neck, through his chest and arms and legs. His foot twitches!

The rumble of indignation resumes with new fervor, and the paralytic almost cries, both at the gathering movement in his feet and the fear that encroaches on him once again. He looks for Jesus, seeking reassurance, because the Pharisees are appalled: Jesus had just claimed to forgive his sin, yet only God can forgive sin.

It is a perfect logical syllogism that Jesus confirms with a miracle. The Pharisees need to understand that reason alone will not serve them in this new Sabbath, because the kingdom of God is built on faith in God's love and mercy and healing. He had just taught these things in the Sermon on the Mount. Now he will demonstrate that his Word has *power*, the power to effect what was spoken. Faith in his Word heals; faith in his love heals. The only obstacle is lack of faith, and the paralytic's friends have plenty of that, even if the paralytic himself is too numb to believe.

Jesus speaks again. "Which is easier to say, 'Your sins are forgiven you,' or to say, 'Rise and walk'?"

I mean, both are easy to *say*, right?

"'But that you may know that the Son of Man has authority on earth to forgive sins'—he said to the man who was paralyzed—'I say to you, rise, take up your bed and go home.'"

Jesus looks the paralytic in the eye, takes his hand, and lifts him up into the new, eternal Sabbath. The kingdom of God has come. It's here. Now.

Are *you* living in it?

The Body Keeps Score

Place yourself into each role: the paralytic who must be carried; the friend who labors with heroic faith for another; Jesus, who is interrupted, yet seizes the opportunity to love; the homeowner whose property is damaged; the crowd who is inconvenienced;

the Pharisee who does not believe in a fantastically merciful, healing, forgiving God. Not like this; not through *him.*

The Gospel of Luke is the most detailed of the synoptic accounts of this healing. The Pharisees had "come from every village of Galilee and Judea and from Jerusalem" in order to test Jesus's credentials. The narrative says that "the power of the Lord was with him to heal." That gives me shivers, because it means the power of the Lord was present to everyone in the vicinity. And yet, according to the account in every gospel, only one received healing that day: the paralytic. And the only reason for his healing was the faith of his friends.

Being paralyzed is a very different condition from blindness or deafness. Spiritually speaking, paralysis is like being stuck in the freeze stress response all the time. Indecision, immobility, stuck-ness, overwhelm, fear, purposelessness, futility, self-medication, repression of anger—they all prevent movement. They're dark and heavy, like paralyzed limbs. They make us feel separated from our bodies, numb, disjointed, checked out.

On the mild end of the spectrum, we experience a form of this dissociation when absorbed in a book or movie, in artistic or creative flow, daydreaming, or highway hypnosis. But when it's in response to stress, trauma, or other forms of suffering, our sense of numbness progresses, causing a freeze response that gets stuck in overdrive. We may develop eating disorders or substance abuse issues, obsessive-compulsive disorder, or unexplained medical conditions. This is the stress response that, when unrelieved, leads to the most physical sickness, because "the body keeps the score," as the best-selling book[2] by the same name showed. The fight-or-flight energy is frozen in the body, and the body becomes dark and sick and heavy.

The Sound Eye

Should we even bother to explore physical healing, since spiritual healing is the primary emphasis of the Bible and salvation?

The body is of little importance, after all, right? Such sentiments surely find their roots in Plato, who said the body is the tomb of the soul; in Docetism, a formal heresy that said Jesus simply "seemed" to have a body; or Gnosticism, another heresy that teaches the body is evil or irrelevant and only the spirit matters.

Although the prophetic books hinted at physical healings to come,[3] in the Old Testament all manner of sickness and illness was thought to be punishment for sin. In the New Testament, we see a deeper revelation arrive in Jesus, who healed bodies and used tangible, physical things to communicate. Jesus's healings and casting out of demons preached kingdom truth. Jesus did not place spiritual realities above physical ones. The Incarnation, Resurrection, and sacraments all show the value Jesus places on the body. The whole point of his coming to live among us was to bring divinity to our humanity.

Mary's assumption takes that emphasis a step further in showing us that rising from the dead and ascending into heaven was not limited to Jesus's own person. As members of his mystical Body, we will rise and ascend in transformation too, because the human person is both spirit and matter, and their union forms a single nature (*CCC*, 365). St. Paul said the body is not a tomb, but a temple (1 Cor 6:19). God heals the whole person. "May the God of peace himself sanctify you wholly; and may your spirit and soul and body be kept sound and blameless at the coming of our Lord Jesus Christ. He who calls you is faithful, and he will do it" (1 Thes 5:23–24).

The gospel, then, is not merely spiritual, moral, philosophical, intellectual, or doctrinal. It's a gospel of the body, too. Incredible, right?

In the Sermon on the Mount, in which Jesus dives deeply into human relationships and behavior, he drops this little nugget on physical healing: "The eye is the lamp of the body. So, if your eye is sound, your whole body will be full of light; but if your eye is not sound, your whole body will be full of darkness.

If then the light in you is darkness, how great is the darkness!" (Mt 6:22–23).

The church fathers understood this "eye" to be the spirit, comprising the heart, soul, and mind.[4] When the heart, soul, and mind are "sound," the body is full of light. Some translations use the words *single* or *clear*, but the idea is oneness, unity, integration, wholeness, and peace. Altogether, this is the very definition of "salvation" and is why Pope Benedict XVI observed, "Healing is an essential dimension of the apostolic mission and of Christian faith in general. When understood at a sufficiently deep level, this expresses the entire content of redemption."[5] If our emotions, memories, judgments, and thoughts are integrated and at peace, rather than fractured and splintered from woundedness, our bodies respond. What might a "body full of light" *feel* like? I bet it feels light, free, and healthy. I bet the healed paralytic knows.

According to current research, 80–95 percent of all physical illnesses are caused by stress.[6] Although the exact percentage is approximated and debated, the mind-body connection is so dramatic and well documented it's not even argued anymore. "Stress" is the catch-all medical term for whatever destabilizes and aggravates the "eye" of a person—his heart, soul, and mind—and therefore affects his body. And is it not pop quizzes, with their painful repetition, increased intensity, inherent historical emotions, dark judgments, fears and lies, and amygdala hijacks, that chronically stress us and cause the most stress?

In the Church, sickness is understood to be "a means of union with Christ and spiritual purification."[7] Working through the physical symptoms that appear in our pop quizzes offers us an opportunity to purify our hearts and seek greater union with Christ and his love.

Fight, Flight, Freeze

Human beings share fight-flee-freeze nervous system responses to stress and trauma with nearly all living creatures, producing the energy needed to fight or flee a predator—or to freeze and play dead—later releasing the energy through trembling, shaking, or licking and grooming.[8]

Unlike animals, humans often store stress or trauma in our bodies, rather than releasing the energy through our nervous system responses.[9] Humans are rational, emotional creatures—and when those emotions manifest in our bodies, according to St. Thomas Aquinas, they are to be ruled by reason in order to help us execute proper, righteous action.[10] They're meant to move us (e–motion). Pop quizzes show us where our emotions are not ruled by reason, but moving us to store destructive, illness-producing tension and trauma.

Humans feel stress emotionally *and* physically. Emotional stress response energy that is not released is stored and "frozen in a kind of suspended animation"[11] that makes itself known in physical symptoms that can become chronic and deadly over time. Physical symptoms can be the body's way of communicating emotional, spiritual, and intellectual dis-ease information. And so, God might be using a pop quiz to show us where our emotions are not ruled by reason, but move us to store tension and trauma in destructive judgments, lies, and self-medicating behaviors.

In *Salvifici Doloris* (*Redemptive Suffering*), St. John Paul II keeps the human spirit-body unity at the forefront by saying we are body-persons. We don't *have* bodies; we *are* bodies. We don't own or wear our bodies or carry them around like a ball and chain; we *are* our bodies, and we are *in* God. The body's powers and abilities are moved or compelled by the spirit's powers and abilities, and vice versa, so that the spirit can suffer when the body is sick. But also, as Jesus said, the eye or spirit is the lamp of the body; when the spirit is one—when the spirit is unified—the whole body is full of light.

Animals don't hold and store trauma. They don't have that capacity because they don't have a rational spirit. For our part, once we become aware that we are holding onto the emotions, judgments, lies, and self-medication of painful memories, we can learn to release pent-up energy that causes sickness. "If you continue in my word . . . you will know the truth, and the truth will make you free" (Jn 8:31–32). We can learn to listen to the body's way of communicating a need for healing, what needs to be healed, and even how to heal through its symptom.

Pop quizzes show us our wounds; they show us what we have chosen to hold onto from the event that we felt to be wounding. We don't choose it consciously or out loud, but we make a choice in response to the event, and we carry that within us. Remember the way we process: Information comes in through the senses, the brain *decides* whether it's dangerous, emotion rises to move us to safety and action, and bodily behavior follows. Automatic stress responses *feel* unmanageable because they are wired in early development and the process happens so fast it feels uncontrollable.

But the biological order of thought > emotion > stress response shows that we retain them—not necessarily from laziness or unwillingness but from ignorance. The spirit (love, intellect, will, emotion) decides. While some say, "the body keeps score," we know that what happens to the body happens to *us*. The decision to retain stress is one we make with the totality of our being. If that's true, then we can also choose to become aware of stress responses and release them in love and to love.

In order to release all that we have held onto from events we felt to be wounding, we first have to be *conscious* of our wounds, judgments, lies, and physical reactions. Helping to draw this awareness into our consciousness is the purpose of the suffering and repetition inherent in pop quizzes, and is why we do not have to go searching for what and where to heal; the Holy Spirit allows pop quizzes for this express purpose. Once we realize that the physical and emotional reactions to certain stimuli are stress or trauma responses, we can begin to consciously release them by working through the pop quizzes—though, depending on the nature and circumstances of the wounds, we may also want or need professional help.

Rather than immediately popping an aspirin, if we made an attempt to listen to our bodies and the symptoms they're producing in a pop quiz, we could discover another cache of helpful self-knowledge. The best way I have found to work through the body section of the Great Commandment in a pop quiz is by following the Bible itself and taking a look at the symptom as a symbol.

Physical Ailments and Their Roots

In *Salvifici Doloris* (*Redemptive Suffering*), St. John Paul the Great pointed out that the Bible "often links 'moral' sufferings with the pain of specific parts of the body: the bones, kidneys, liver, viscera, heart. In fact, one cannot deny that moral sufferings have a 'physical' or somatic element, and that they are often reflected in the state of the entire organism." Perhaps it's useful to read that again: "Moral sufferings . . . are often reflected in the state of the entire organism," he says. What, then, can physical symptoms tell us about an "unsound eye," how to heal, and how God is healing us—heart, soul, mind, and strength?

Because we need grace in order for nature to heal in this way, we ask the Holy Spirit in his presence: *What is this physical symptom in my body communicating? How does this symptom "help" me? What seems to be its role?*

For instance, in my previous example about the surgeon with the unexplained sickness, his symptoms were messages from his body. Chronic fatigue made him too "sick and tired" to follow through with insincere commitments. Remember that we do not have bodies; we are our bodies. Since he felt unable to speak truthfully for himself out of fear of disappointing others, his body spoke for him. When I began to ask questions about what the sickness was communicating and its role in his life, he called it his "precious," because he felt it was killing him, yet seemed unable to do away with its "help." When he learned to speak authentically, when his communication and relationships were established on truth "in the inward parts" (Ps 51:6, NKJV), his body responded.

Here in the West, we have all the comforts and innumerable means to make ourselves immediately comfortable. Additionally, we tend toward a gnostic view of the body that makes it more of an irritation or necessary evil than a gift, especially when it's not cooperating in health and ease. When the "eye" of the body, or the spirit (heart, soul, mind), is suffering, we self-medicate and numb until we are sick. When the body no longer "cooperates" with us, when it is in pain or dis-ease, we attempt to force it into immediate submission with further drugs and external interventions, *without any attempt to listen to what it's communicating*. Don't external interventions that are unaccompanied by a search for possible interior stimuli often prove frustratingly temporary and offer mediocre relief, if they are helpful at all?

I can almost hear you saying: *Sonja, peoples' bodies aren't always communicating something! Just because it picked up a virus or has been bitten by a tick and might be feeling the effects years later, it's silly to navel-gaze and try to "learn something" from one's body. Cancer and other dread diseases are also not our fault and aren't trying to tell us something about our inner life!*

I get it. What I am proposing is mostly new to the Church and feels fearfully radical or medieval after decades of modern medicine, pharmacology, and New Ageism have conditioned us to distrust such things. But at the same time, modern medicine is telling us that 80–95 percent of our physical issues are caused by stress. Our culture wants us to think in terms of a false dichotomy, in which our bodies and spirits are separate realities, which eliminates the possibility of seeing the truth of physical problems that *are* rooted in emotional, spiritual, or psychological problems.[12]

So, what do we have to lose by listening to and respecting the wonder of our bodies while we're seeking external treatment? What if we simply turned our attention to the symptoms in our pop quizzes the way the Great Commandment leads us to do? After hundreds of one-on-one spiritual consultations, I can tell you that integrating the heart, soul, mind, and body with the Holy Spirit *always* leads to illumination, greater insight, wholeness, and peace.

Ultimately, aging and deterioration are inevitable. Illness, disease, and death are not always the effect of stress or sin; they are also tied to the effects of the Fall and are part of the human condition. If that were not the case, we could skip the doctor and go straight to the confessional, expecting to come out completely well. Even those who were directly healed by Christ died, and we will die, of course, in order that God can fulfill our final healing union with himself.

But the consequences of sin—the sin we are born into, sins we commit, and those committed against us—impact creation in often mysterious ways, just as God's love does. What *if* we can be more vital and fruitful, now, and even while we age? "They will still bring forth fruit in old age, they are ever full of sap and green" (Ps 92:14). Integrating our bodies and spirits offers us dynamism and potency while we age. Our bodies "know" when we're not right inside. Seeking union with God always brings healing and wholeness of one kind or another. To believe otherwise is to discount the Lord who "heals all your diseases" (Ps 103:3).

When I suggest to people outside of consultations who have physical issues—even minor ones—that we listen to our bodies, they often resist or misunderstand me. They hear the suggestion as absurd, an accusation of laziness, shame or blame for their sickness, or simplistic medieval stupidity. They think I either want to comfort them or show them how to have a more positive attitude. They don't get that releasing negative emotions in healthy, safe ways is necessary for their health; that forgiveness is a spiritual requirement for healing; that continuing to live out of the judgments and lies they have come to believe about themselves and others will perpetuate their problems, physically and otherwise.

But those with whom I work in consultations know what I'm saying is true from their healing experiences. Emotional toxicity is communicated through the body. In fact, the body is always communicating information, because it's always emoting and thinking! Working through pop quizzes, when accompanied by appropriate external treatments and other lifestyle changes that address physical issues from an external point of view, frees us to love with every part of the human person: heart, soul, mind, and strength. After all,

> The Lord created medicines out of the earth, and the sensible will not despise them. Was not water made sweet with a tree in order that his power might be known? And he gave skill to men that he might be glorified in his marvelous works. By them he heals and takes away pain; the pharmacist makes of them a compound. His works will never be finished; and from him health is upon the face of the earth.
>
> My son, when you are sick do not be negligent, but pray to the Lord, and he will heal you. Give up your faults and direct your hands aright, and cleanse your heart from all sin. Offer your sweet-smelling sacrifice, and a memorial portion of fine flour, and pour oil on your offering, as much as you can afford. And give the physician his place, for the Lord created him; let him not leave you, for there is need of him. there is a time when success lies in the hands of the physicians. (Sir 38:4–13)

When we are ill, the passage instructs, we must address love deficits in heart, soul, and mind, *and* we "give the doctor his place." Healing requires both spirit *and* body—both interior intervention *and* external intervention—because the body knows how to heal, and it also stores all of your experiences and expresses all of them.

Certainly our environment can threaten our well-being. Air, water, medicines, clothing, homes, DNA—everything is full of toxins. Chronic physical, emotional, spiritual, or mental stress or abuse hinder the body's ability to eliminate such toxins. Still, the human immune system is a wonder. Who knows how radically God might heal us, inside out—even if our sickness is related to hereditary or environmental factors—if we were to deeply orient our hearts, souls, minds, and bodies to him in love?

Certainly we are born into a world full of sin, suffering, sickness, and death, and all of that should be an entry point for God in our lives and hearts and a means of deeper union with him. After all, "suffering unleashes love." Remember also that research shows 80–95 percent of physical issues have emotional and spiritual components; so that leaves 5–20 percent that do not have psychological, emotional, or spiritual origins. Still, what if God *wants* to manifest his love to us by restoring our bodies through a process of healing love in our hearts, souls, and minds? What if there's more we can and *should* do than "offer it up"? What could it hurt to consider how our spirits might be influencing our bodies? How much time, money, and stress could we save ourselves if we simply considered the biblical links between moral sufferings and physical suffering that St. John Paul II pointed out, to see if they might be relevant to our own symptoms?

Perhaps you'd like to ask the Holy Spirit to illuminate any heart, soul, and mind issues that might be underlying your physical symptoms. Remember that when God speaks *to* you, he's speaking *about* you; the primary subject here, and in all your pop quizzes, is you, not other people. It can also help to know *how* the Bible associates certain parts of the body with spiritual symbolism. I get far more deeply into these connections and possible resolutions in the Love Heals Masterclass.[13] But the Bible's associations between spirit and body can be clues, so that in listening to what your body might be communicating in a pop quiz, you will experience the wonder of it as the gift it is and live through it more incarnationally.

For example, I've learned that my minor, recurring neck pain can be a signal that I am being unconsciously stubborn in some area of my life. Sure, my posture is not always ergonomically correct when I sit at my desk, but experimenting with physical pains, in my pop quizzes and otherwise, has revealed a tendency to assert my will in ways that manifest in my neck. I also know that stinging in my upper back between my shoulder blades indicates some unconscious self-sufficiency in my responsibilities that I have not invited Jesus into to "shoulder" with me. The pain is a distraction from unconscious—but important—emotions, judgments, and thoughts. Every time I have listened to my body, I have learned something important. When I acknowledge its message, the pain disappears. Whether fear or love, our bodies communicate through pain, dis-ease, and healing.

The body is made to worship, to communicate healing information, and to possess its own internal healing mechanisms. Even if we've been abused by ourselves or others, even if we do not like how we look or feel at the moment, our bodies are sacred and precious in the eyes of God. Why else would Jesus elevate the body in his Incarnation and Resurrection?

Your Body Matters

Whatever body baggage we bring to our worship of God in trying to get to know who he is and what he's like, and trying to learn to love him with all of our heart, soul, mind, and strength, we have to remember that our bodies are holy, too, and they matter to him. We can learn to love our bodies, no matter what they look like, no matter what shape they're in due to aging, trauma, pregnancies, weight, or abuse.

I once made a body comment that accidentally lit up my private social media community: "Jesus is not white, y'all." And he isn't. The comment wasn't surprising or irritating for most people, but someone was annoyed enough to reply, "It doesn't even matter. It doesn't matter what race Jesus is."

She wasn't wrong, since Jesus came to establish a universal Church. The word *Catholic* means universal—all tribes, nations, races, and tongues. But perhaps she wasn't *right* either. Race and culture matter to each one of us because they are important parts of our identities—and we know Jesus came to share every part of our humanity. It matters what race Jesus is not because his experience elevates one race above another but because it elevates *every* race. Jesus came from a particular race in a specific time and place, elevating every race, time, and place.

I made my first trip to the Holy Land with a group of people I had never met. It felt so monumental for me to be walking in the footsteps of Jesus in the land they call the Fifth Gospel, because when you're there, the scriptures come alive. You never have to wonder again where these stories took place; you stand in them; you smell them and touch them and hear them. You know Jesus was there; you walk the trails that Jesus walked from the valleys to the hills and from town to town.

One of our first stops was the Sea of Galilee, which we crossed in what they call a "Jesus boat," singing to the praise music blaring from speakers in the stern. I took a moment away from the group and walked to the bow, and sort of did that whole Titanic thing where I had my hands raised, praising God, listening to the music, thanking him for the trip that someone had given me as a surprise gift.

As I stood there, enjoying God and all he had tenderly provided, he said into my heart, "I just wanted you to see my place." I was so struck by that! I thought, *Oh my goodness, of course!* Of course Jesus has a place, and of course, he loves it! It is special to him because it's "home."

I came to realize that his place matters, because his body matters. Your body matters because he created it as a place for his spirit. Your body is a tabernacle, or temple, of God. Yet, if your body has experienced abuse—violence, neglect, disrespect, dishonor—you may develop a negative view of your body. You may believe your body is not part of the "real you" or that it's a sort of ball and chain that you're dragging around. I'd like to invite you to begin considering your body as the gift that it is. Perhaps it was abused. Likely it's been hurt. Possibly it was neglected. And yes, it can manifest the pain in your heart, your mind, and your soul. But that is a gift in itself.

Your body—all of it, gender, race, shape, and ability—is a gift. No matter how it has been maligned, no matter how much you may malign it. It is God's tabernacle, and therefore it is holy. It is not a husk that you'll drag around till you're dead, when you can finally be released from it and go be with God in your soul . . . don't fall into that Gnosticism. Be thankful for your body. Be thankful that your body was given to you to receive, to learn, to know God and to worship him, and to love. Experiencing your body this way can be a way to begin to heal from race, abuse, and neglect issues that you've experienced in your body. Your body is you. It is your friend.

It's impossible to be physically healthy when you hate your body. Whatever the root causes—media, trauma, pregnancies, abuse, aging, bullying—how a person perceives her appearance and feels in her body directly impacts her physical health. What is the truth about your body?

Here is an utterly beautiful truth that we should cling to in moments we are tempted to hate our bodies:

> The human body shares in the dignity of "the image of God": it is a human body precisely because it is animated by a spiritual soul, and it is the whole human person that is intended to become, in the body of Christ, a temple of the Spirit: Man, though made of body and soul, is a unity. Through his very bodily condition he sums up in himself the elements of the material world. Through him they are thus brought to their highest perfection and can raise their voice in praise freely given to the Creator. For this reason,

man may not despise his bodily life. Rather he is obliged to regard his body as good and to hold it in honour since God has created it and will raise it up on the last day. (*CCC*, 364)

By the power of the Eucharist (Jn 6:54 and *CCC*, 1524), the body you now bear will be raised in resurrection and changed into a spiritual body (*CCC*, 999). Our bodies are that important. Your body is a temple for the Spirit, a woven veil that covers the presence of God who rests on the throne of your heart.

The Body as a Sacred Covering

The word used in the Old Testament to describe the woven veil hiding the presence of God from human eyes in the Holy of Holies is *sakak* in Hebrew, meaning "covered" or "screened."[14] The word *sakak* is used almost exclusively in scripture to describe the veiling of the presence of God in the Old Testament Tabernacle in the priests and Holy of Holies, with a notable exception: when David uses this word to describe how we were woven together secretly by God.

Psalm 139:15 rejoices, "My frame was not hidden from thee, when I was being made in secret." Earlier in the chapter, verse 13 marvels, "Thou didst form my inward parts, thou didst knit me together in my mother's womb." The word "knit" is *sakak*, also sometimes translated in this verse as "wove" or "woven" to be a "covering."

The psalmist used this word to describe his own flesh, stating in the most delicate poetry that his body, your body, was prepared to veil the presence of God—that each one's anatomy should become the tabernacle of God. He personally knit together every soul and body with the express intention that it should become a home for himself. In fact, while the body is the product of procreation between a man, woman, and God, "the Church teaches that every soul is created immediately by God—it is not 'produced' by the parents" (*CCC*, 365). Your soul—your personality, temperament, gifts, talents—was created personally and directly by God. What a wonder! What respect! What dignity! What love! "Do you not know that your body is the temple of the Holy Spirit within you, which you have from God? . . . So glorify God in your body" (1 Cor 6:19–20).

The RSV2CE translation of Psalm 139:13–14 reads, in part, "I am wondrously made. Wonderful are your works!" The New King James Version of the Bible I grew up with is slightly different: "You covered me in my mother's womb. I will praise you; for I am fearfully *and* wonderfully made." In this translation, the word "covered" is *sakak*, the word we mentioned earlier that is used in scripture almost exclusively to describe the veil. The word *fearfully* means "reverently, respectfully." I am formed with reverence and respect.

What a tender thought.

What does it mean to make something respectfully? God is an artist, the ultimate artist. When my mother cross-stitches vintage samplers, she does not just grab random threads and linens and begin arbitrarily sewing. If an artist creates something respectfully, she takes the time to plan, she thinks through each stitch and step, and she counts carefully. She has chosen a particular pattern and knows what it will look like before she even starts sewing.

An artist might intend to convey a specific statement or emotion through what he creates, or he may desire to inspire awe or an appreciation for beauty or an idea. But his work is premeditated, designed. Once the work is complete, he does not throw it away, because it communicates something; the artist has left part of himself there. More so than any human artist, God never clones a work; it is unrepeatable. Just like a masterpiece, God makes each person with a specific plan to accomplish certain things and convey certain messages, as described by St. John Henry Newman:

> God has created me to do him some definite service. He has committed some work to me which he has not

> committed to another. I have my mission—I never may know it in this life, but I shall be told it in the next... I am a link in a chain, a bond of [connection] between persons. He has not created me for naught. I shall do good, I shall do his work; I shall be an angel of peace, a preacher of truth in my own place, while not intending it, if I do but keep his commandments and serve in my calling. Therefore, I will trust him.
>
> Whatever, wherever I am, I can never be thrown away. If I am in sickness, my sickness may serve him, in perplexity, my perplexity may serve him; if I am in sorrow, my sorrow may serve him.... He does nothing in vain.... He knows what he is about. He may take away my friends, he may throw me among strangers, he may make me feel desolate, make my spirits sink, hide my future from me—still he knows what he is about.[15]

Just visit a zoo. One thing that strikes you about creation is its diversity. God loves differentness. Even among a field of daisies, there are differences in height, leaf structure, vibrancy of petal and stamen color, location, and neighboring weeds.

The saints are also distinct. Even if they are similar in temperament or personality or historical setting, there is no single pattern of holiness, no one way of following Christ. Each of these was dissimilar, but all are one in Christ. Each found sanctity by reflecting some aspect of the divine reality in simply being who and what they were made so reverently and respectfully to be. We cannot imitate any of them exactly, or else we do a disservice to the reverence and respect with which *we* were made and the purpose we are meant to fulfill.

No one can follow God's plan for my life, because no one else has the same strengths, weaknesses, interests, abilities, quirks, experiences, environment, or opportunities that are unique to me. I am called to give myself away in love in ways that you are not. And the thing is, I am unable to do that at all if I do not embrace who I am in soul and body.

Of course, I will wander from my true nature, sometimes in ignorance, sometimes on purpose; that's called sin, which opposes God and ourselves. But not even sin can prevent me from my God-ordained purpose so long as I keep my eyes on Christ: not Adam's sin, not personal sin, and not the eternal consequences of sin. All that's left is to wrestle with suffering, illness, death, frailty, and the tendency to sin, but none of that can harm those who do not consent to the temptation to sin or despair but resist through the graces of Christ (see *CCC*, 1263–1264). God defines me. He has ordained my fearful and wonderful nature.

I must not try to imitate any one saint exactly. I can look to them all, studying their unique holiness, but then I must allow that specific reverence God wants to express through me to come forward.

I am respectfully and wonderfully made—spirit and body—woven together like the Tabernacle curtain at the entrance to the Holy of Holies. By simply being wholly and fully myself, minus sin, my body is a holy veil that shelters yet announces the presence of Christ.

Love Blockers: Sugar and Anger

Now that we are clear that our bodies are as holy as our souls, we can reconsider that our most deeply rooted, destructive habits against our bodies also come from a deficit of love. We've been told since we were children to eat real, healthy foods, to exercise, and to get plenty of water and restful sleep to support good physical health. We spoke at length in the previous chapters about healing stress responses and reducing stress in love; we acknowledged that hereditary and environmental factors in disease and sickness are real and destructive; and we emphasized that personal responsibility for our emotional, mental, spiritual, and physical health does not equal blame.

All of what nurtures physical health is well-traversed ground that does not need to be rehashed here, except the point that we do not take as good care of our bodies as we should because we lack authentic love for ourselves. So I'd like to point out two blocks[16] to physical healing that you've likely not thought about in spiritual terms: sugar and anger.

According to attachment theory, the deepest human pain is separation[17] from love. When we feel deprived or separated from love in our lives, through death, alienation, judgment, loss, unforgiveness, or isolation, we often turn to or seek depersonalized substitutes such as sugar, sex, and alcohol to temporarily and artificially elevate the "happy hormones" or "love chemicals": dopamine, serotonin, oxytocin, and endorphins. Because love is the primary human need, and our self-medicating coping mechanisms for unmet love needs were learned and wired into the brain during early development, these mechanisms override conscious intention. Fortunately, once we become aware of what's going on, we can seek the Holy Spirit's healing love in the strength part of our pop quizzes.

Sugar as a Substitute for Love

All of us have self-medicating tendencies—whether physical or emotional, as in sugar or anger—but we also know they actively change the chemistry of the body and compound dis-ease. Modern foods and other environmental substances contain additional toxic chemicals that keep the body in a constant state of stress. Sugar is a particularly powerful hit of dopamine, serotonin, and endorphins into the system.

"Looking for love in all the wrong places," as the country song goes, is not good for you physically, and it's not good for you spiritually or emotionally, either. Attachment to something apart from God cannot and will never satisfy the deep primary hunger for authentic love that we all have, while temporary substitutes mask the deficit of love and how to get that need met.

Human beings must have love. Dopamine, serotonin, oxytocin, and endorphin hormones are necessary for development—physically, emotionally, spiritually, and mentally. When we can't or don't socialize, touch, exercise, pray, eat, or sleep properly, our love chemicals become deficient, and we try to satiate the need elsewhere.

And that's why you can't seem to break that self-medicating habit.

Pop quizzes trigger a stress response and often tempt us to gravitate toward self-medication and addictions. Food addictions are particularly difficult, in part, because we must consistently feed ourselves in order to stay alive. But sugar, including carbs and alcohol, supplies an artificial dump of love chemicals. When we're stuck in a fear response, we cannot grow out of the habit and cannot simply stop. Shame, self-loathing, and condemnation surround self-medicating habits so that the cycle continues, and we remain paralyzed.

What if, instead, we sought the "eye" of the symptom with Christ? What if we asked the Holy Spirit for help in understanding the root of it and learning how to outgrow it? If we do not do this deeper work now, the same needs will resurface later in life, shocking and surprising us with their vehemence.[18] As St. Paul says in his letter to the Romans, "For I know that nothing good dwells within me, that is, in my flesh. I can will what is right, but I cannot do it. For I do not do the good I want, but the evil I do not want is what I do. Now if I do what I do not want, it is no longer I that do it, but sin which dwells within me" (Rom 7:18–20).

Again, *flesh* here is a reference to concupiscence, our tendency toward choosing what is sinful or harmful. Paul is not disparaging the human body; he's saying there's a tendency toward sin that causes him to act in ways that contradict his faith due to an unhealed "eye" of the body: the heart, soul, and mind. Perhaps it's even his "thorn . . . in the flesh" (2 Cor 12:7).

St. Paul was no "baby Christian" at the time of this writing; he had experienced one of the most powerful, healing revelations of Christ's love recorded in the Bible. The Letter to the Romans, in which he stated his body-spirit contradiction, is thought to have been written about halfway through his ministry. So he was no rookie in faith or healing, yet he was still battling some deep-seated wounds. His struggle should give us great hope along with Paul himself, who offered the assurance of God's love, even there, in the lowest behaviors of the body: "Walk in the Spirit, and you shall not fulfill the lust of the flesh" (Gal 5:16–17, NKJV).

Self-control is a fruit of the Spirit (Gal 5:23) and temperance is a virtue, but if self-medicating habits are physical symptoms of something deeper, shouldn't we go deeper, too? Have you discovered how powerless you are in the face of a self-medicating habit? What if listening to our bodies' need for love and directing that neediness to the infinite abyss of God's eternal love is the key to healing such physical attachments, however strong or mild?

Love heals. We learn to love ourselves and others authentically with healthy boundaries. We are loved in authentic love relationships with spouses and children and friends. Yet they are not enough, are they? We must reach for divine love personally and specifically because only God can satisfy the bottomless pit of neediness for love with which he created the human person. Other people cannot do it. They don't have the degree or amount of love to give to satisfy another person's "infinite abyss." Blaise Pascal said it beautifully:

> What else does this craving, and this helplessness, proclaim but that there was once in man a true happiness, of which all that now remains is the empty print and trace? This he tries in vain to fill with everything around him, seeking in things that are not there the help he cannot find in those that are, though none can help, since this infinite abyss can be filled only with an infinite and immutable object; in other words by God himself.[19]

We *can* grow out of this dependence, these attachments to things and people, that cannot satisfy our deepest, primary need.

Stress and anxiety produce fear and anxiety alarms that remain in us unless and until we process them properly in love.

Strength to STOP

When we become aware that God is sending us a pop quiz, we can use the STOP Tool to prevent falling into the bag of chips or the French fries, the box of wine or the carbs. The STOP Tool helps us to love God with all our strength. I can direct myself to God, fully process the pop quiz, offer the right sacrifice in charity for myself and the other, and rest with him in prayer where I can receive authentic love, rather than seeking the substitute that will not satiate me.

Sugar is a powerfully addictive substance in almost everything we eat. Like most love substitutes, it provides a temporary jolt of dopamine, serotonin, and oxytocin; this only solidifies and strengthens our dependence. These substitutes for God's healing love also compound the physical damage and prevent physical healing. Whenever we become attached to these substitutes, we turn them into idols and cease seeking satisfaction in God, depending on created things to fill a love-space that God has created for himself.

Ultimately, these attachment hungers do serve a purpose. We're looking for authentic love, because attachment or the need for love is a primary need. At first, you don't have control over it; you don't even know it when it's happening. But once you have the awareness, you can start to see your pattern and what you gravitate toward on a regular basis. That's why we are looking at our pop quizzes and our body's natural responses in them: stress responses, physical symptoms, and self-medicating habits.

What self-medicating habit do you gravitate toward when trying to satiate a need for love? When you experience separation in lack of love or judgment, are you not automatically drawn to that thing? Sugar and other self-medications are barriers or strongholds against healing—physical healing, but healing in general—because they become idols. We cannot muscle through them; we must outgrow them, because the need for love overrides all conscious intention.

We become aware of the cycle through our pop quizzes; working with the Holy Spirit, we put a strategy in place for a different response to our triggers; we resist the substitute. We move from fight-flight-freeze to safety and maturation. If you don't have an alternative to your self-medicating habit or your sugar, whatever it is, if you don't have a true love attachment, you will never kick the habit, because it's just a substitute for the real thing, an idol, a destructive attachment.

This is why the saints preach detachment as a constant *process*, because we gravitate toward created things to try to fill that primary human need for love when deprived of love. Proper (secure) attachments are first and primarily to God himself: "Love the Lord with all your heart, and with all your soul, and with all your mind, and with all your strength" (Mk 12:30). Then we must have a healthy attachment to and love for ourselves. Only then can we maintain healthy attachments to others, ones in which we're not pretending we don't need others (stoicism) or trying to suck the energy out of other people and things (leeching). They don't have enough love to give us, and created things can never love us, either. St. Thomas Aquinas was clear that we cannot love God or our neighbor if we do not love ourselves in an ordered way.

The Eucharist Is the Power of the Resurrection, a Place at the Table

I worked with a woman who had what she called "food noise" that prevented a healthy grasp on food and her body image. She ate secretly, overate, hid food, self-soothed with food, and frequently ate fast food and junk food on the way home. She substituted food for love. Her body was understandably sick and tired.

By the time she began working with me, she had gotten a lot of help through therapy, counseling, and nutritionists but still had not broken her disordered attachment to food; she had not found a proper substitute. She had a real relationship with God but wasn't truly and consistently tapping into his loving presence on a moment-by-moment basis when triggered by pop quizzes, which provoked separation anxiety and deprivation of love.

She shared that in her family she never felt like she had a place at the table; she always felt like an outsider. It was fascinating to me that she used the language of the table, because she also commented that the Eucharist was her favorite thing. I shared that the Eucharist is the power of the Resurrection (Jn 6:54 and *CCC*, 1524). I asked, *How might Jesus raise your body out of this self-medicating habit and heal it through more frequent reception of the Eucharist, right now*? I posed the suggestion: *What if, for the next forty days, you eat only in communion with other people?*

She was alone by herself at lunch on a daily basis, so I suggested attending Mass, where she can receive true communion in the Eucharist and her seat at the table is always open; she can also experience God's nourishing love and physical touch in communion. She exchanged the lie that there's no place for her at the table with the truth that she has a seat at the Eucharistic table by virtue of her Baptism and Confirmation. Jesus satiates her need for both food and love.

The church fathers say that the way to break the fleshly hold of an idol rooted in wounds is to crucify the flesh (Gal 5:24). Because sometimes we have hardwired coping mechanisms from childhood, we may never completely erase them while in our bodies. Instead, we hold them in tension, crucified with Christ (Gal 2:20): authentic love on the right, temptations in pop quizzes on the left; heaven above, earth below. We are crucified with Christ until reborn in resurrection.

We bring the flesh under subjection by digging to the root with the Holy Spirit in our pop quizzes, thereby replacing the idol with the real thing. The real thing for the woman with the "food noise" and for all of us is available at "the one table" of the Lord (*CCC*, 103), where we are fed by scripture and the Eucharist and receive the bread of life, the physical love of God, and the power of the body's resurrection and healing.

Suppressed Anger Blocks Healing Love

Through experience with spiritual consultations, I have found that people with the freeze stress response (paralysis) are often the sickest, usually because they are also the most angry or resentful while also living in denial of such emotions. Anger kills, and is a block to healing: "Does a man harbor anger against another, and yet seek healing from the Lord?" (Sir 28:3).

Many Christians were raised to believe that anger is a sin, so they've spent their lives repressing anger in order to please authority figures and God. They believe anger is a lack of charity. Since they never explode in displays of anger, many stubbornly insist they are never angry at all until I use the words bitterness and resentment. Almost to a person, when asked their greatest fear, they say "hell." Why?

Often such personalities are naturally sweet, serene, and agreeable, and they highly value a lack of conflict. Frequently, they are pleasers and caretakers. They have few or no boundaries in what they will do for others or tolerate from them in "charity." They wouldn't dare be overtly angry with someone, partly because they often experienced a parent who scared them with anger and partly because they cannot tolerate others being angry with them. And they would surely never admit they are angry at God for fear they will go to hell. I always ask, *Do you think he doesn't know you're angry at him? Do you think you're hiding it?*

After spending decades of going-along-to-get-along, serving others generously and even heroically, and being easy to be with, we may have developed an unconscious habit of hiding bitterness and resentment against those who have wounded us, against those who have taken advantage of us—and even against God himself for allowing us to be repeatedly exploited. Because we believe we have always acted with charity toward others, we might surmise God is punishing us despite our goodness.

But these are all projections.

The truth is, we are partly responsible for what we allow through a lack of boundaries. When we suspect exploitation, we should erect a boundary—or assist in protecting victims of exploitation—if we can.

We often serve others when it is best not to, for us *or* them. Vanity, fear of being disliked, and worry that we will be thought of poorly push us to give more of ourselves than is healthy or charitable. Or perhaps we are generous out of pride in feeling superior to others through our visible good works. That's not love; that's fear. And it's a whitewashed tomb hiding the rottenness of bitterness and resentment. Why are you passive aggressive? Because you are angry and haven't learned to "let the puppy pee safely."

In my experience, people who are highly agreeable while also extremely conscientious and orderly often notice and feel their pop quizzes physically, first, because they have a habit of stuffing strong emotions such as anger (although they usually feel resentment if asked to discern). They are often afraid to *feel* strongly; they are afraid they will displease others by reacting or overreacting. If this is you, it can be helpful and even necessary to discover that your pop quizzes typically manifest in a physical "flare-up," rather than an emotional one, and to begin working through your pop quizzes with the strength part of the STOP Tool.

"The godless in heart cherish anger; they do not cry for help when he binds them" (Job 36:13). This verse suggests that cherishing anger—bitterness and resentment—leads to a lack of spiritual awareness and to disconnection from God. But along with paralyzing self-medications such as sugar, repressing anger also disconnects us from ourselves *and our bodies*. Putting on the happy face when making decisions out of fear that are contrary to good boundaries and authentic love builds resentment, bitterness, and disease. Anger eats us up inside—it can lead to chronic inflammation of our bodies in severe autoimmune responses,[20] disease,[21] and pain[22]—and therefore blocks healing.

Anger is a necessary human emotion, and almost always follows a pop quiz, because we feel unjustly treated. Therefore, we need to know how to express anger—verbally, as we spoke about in chapter 2, but also physically—so we can release fight-or-flight stress energy that becomes frozen in our bodies when we are paralyzed from social or religious fears.

Because my anger was often explosive in my early life, I was comfortable expressing it physically while learning to do so more charitably, safely, and privately. For those who abhor physical aggression of any sort, allowing one's body to express anger will be harder, but sometimes the physical component is crucial to allowing your body to express fight-or-flight energy so it's not stored in your body, as Peter Levine pointed out in his book *Waking the Tiger*.[23] Perhaps it's even more crucial for those who have suppressed anger in their bodies over long periods of time. At the very least, we *must* learn to acknowledge anger and express it with God. Let the puppy pee!

Addressing physical symptoms and expressing the range of human emotions safely and charitably—especially when working through pop quizzes—is part of how we love the Lord with all our strength. His love can help us "rise and walk" out of stress responses, self-medicating behaviors, dis-ease, and anger that have paralyzed us for years.

Let's Review

- I love the Lord with all my heart, soul, mind, and strength by cooperating with him in the pop quizzes he allows and by using the STOP Tool.
- In the T step of the STOP Tool, I love God with all my *heart* by expressing everything in my heart regarding my pop quizzes, identifying the main *emotion* in the pop quiz and the *memory* or memories associated with that emotion.

- In the T step of the STOP Tool, I love God with all my *soul* by telling God all the *judgments* I find in my soul, allowing the Holy Spirit to pour his *forgiveness* and mercy into them, and forgiving myself and my wounder(s).
- In the T step of the STOP Tool, I love the Lord with all my *mind* by refuting *lies*, negativity, and fear of deprivation with the *truth* of God's Word and applying it to my life.
- If my spirit is whole, my body will be "full of light" (Mt 6:22–23).
- I don't have a body; I am an embodied person. My body is as holy as my spirit.
- At least 80 percent of physical sicknesses and diseases have emotional and spiritual roots.
- My body does not store stress *for* me; I hold my wounds in. Physical symptoms can convey information and self-knowledge.
- In the T step of the STOP Tool, I love the Lord with all my *strength* by listening to the *physical symptoms* my body expresses when stressed in my pop quizzes.

Invitation

In the last chapter's Invitation section, I shared one of my pop quizzes involving my husband's "gift of criticism" and my rebellion. I have used the STOP Tool since my twenties, so many years have coalesced my pop quizzes into what I now call a "constellation"—a recognizable, familiar grouping-together of symptoms that helps me navigate. It's always the same wounded emotions and memories (heart), judgments and forgiveness (soul), lies (mind), and tight chest with difficulty breathing (strength) for me, and they are repetitive.

Once you become familiar with your own constellation, all your pop quizzes will center around it for some time, giving you practice in charity, boundaries, and virtue (offering the right sacrifice) and deepening your intimacy with God until your healing is as deep as the wound. Identifying the heart, soul, mind, and strength constellation allows you to largely skim those parts because they're the same or similar every time. At that point, you only need to Sin not, Tell God, Offer the right sacrifice, and Put your trust in him.

But *working through* the strength part of the pop quiz was relatively new to me, then, and caught me completely by surprise. The tight chest, pounding heart, and difficulty breathing in my pop quizzes were familiar symptoms, but I had never gone deeper than acknowledging them. I hadn't known I could.

At the time, I was offering a podcast series on physical healing called *Somata*.[24] I had been exploring the Church's theology and teachings on physical healing throughout Church history, modern research on the mind-body connection and physical health, healing trauma through somatic therapies, and current practices for healing in the Church. I discovered the somatic element that St. John Paul II spoke of in *Salvifici Doloris* (*Redemptive Suffering*) in a new way, as information we *need* and that God created our bodies to produce for healing.

I was sitting in my office researching and prepping for an episode of my podcast when I felt the Holy Spirit use what I was learning to give me insight into a recent pop quiz. I had failed to practice temperance in a situation with my husband, who was angry and giving me the silent treatment. I felt silly, but decided to listen for what my body might be saying in my pop quiz. Thinking about the situation, I felt my chest squeezing and my heart pounding until I couldn't breathe easily. I knew the lie was "badness," as it always was, and reminded myself of all my experiences of my heavenly Father's love and tenderness even when I was "bad."

I asked the Holy Spirit if there was something more, and I placed a hand on my heart, rubbing it in circles.[25] It felt so awkward then, but I really tuned into my body and what I might learn from the familiar symptoms. And the memory of standing on tiptoe in front of that bedroom door with my nose pressed against it for hours leaped immediately to my mind. Not surprising; that's a familiar memory. But when I probed for the action my body seemed automatically urged to perform, I about fell out of my chair. I saw my "little self" shoving violently away from the door, yelling, "I am NOT bad! I am NOT BAD!"

I am tearful again as I write this, because as silly as I felt, in the privacy of my office, I did that very thing. I pushed my face against the wall as the tears fell, I drew my arms up, and I shoved against the wall, over and over, yelling hoarsely, "I am NOT bad! I am NOT BAD!"

Part of what was so shocking about my almost immediate response to listening to my body was the strength of the response and how good it felt. Although I know I experienced trauma as a child, it was long-term and mostly emotional, and does not compare to others who have experienced far, far worse. Maybe that's you. What are you holding in your body?

If you're not ready to know, take comfort in the reality that "the nervous system is constantly self-regulating, so what you can't process today will still be there when you do feel ready, when you feel stronger, more resourceful and capable."[26] If you do feel ready, perhaps you'd like to try it.

Benediction—LOVE the Word®

L | Listen (Receive the Word.)

Psalm 4:4–5 (RSV2CE): "Be angry, but sin not; commune with your own hearts on your beds, and be silent. Offer right sacrifices, and put your trust in the Lord."

S—Sin not;

T—Tell God everything in your heart, soul, mind, and strength;

O—Offer the right sacrifice;

P—Put your trust in God.

O | Observe (Observe your relationships and circumstances.)

With the Holy Spirit and in his presence, think back to your latest pop quiz. Try to place yourself back into the situation, remembering with all your senses.[27] Without judgment, observe whether you sinned or not (S). Remembering that the T step is a reference to the *Shema,* tell God everything in your heart, soul, mind, and strength.

Heart: *What is the main emotion I am feeling or felt? What is the memory behind this emotion and the symptoms I'm experiencing? When is the first time I can remember feeling exactly this way?*

Stay here until a memory surfaces, asking the Holy Spirit to reveal it. When you have a memory or memories, move to the soul.

Soul: *What do I feel in my heart about the person in my immediate pop quiz and the person in my wounded memory who hurt me? What is the judgment I made or am making about these people? How is this judgment a projection of my own fault or inferiority?*

Remembering that forgiveness is the cancellation of a debt, forgive your wounders: *In the Name of Jesus, I forgive _____ for _____*. Remember to forgive yourself, too. Perhaps you'd like to visualize bringing your wounder(s) to the foot of the Cross and leaving them there.

Mind: *Holy Spirit, what is the lie or lies I came to believe about myself in this event? Holy Spirit, what is the truth you want to exchange with me for that lie?*

Stay here until you hear from the Holy Spirit, asking him to reveal it. If you need help, thumb through the truths I compiled for you in the back of the Working through Pop Quizzes Workbook. When you have both the lie and the truth, renounce the lie(s) and announce the truth:

In the Name of Jesus, I renounce the lie that . . .

In the Name of Jesus, I announce the truth that . . .

Strength: As you relive the pop quiz, notice how your body feels. *Where do I feel this pop quiz in my body? What is my body telling me through these symptoms? What action does my body want to take right now? Is there a self-defense action my body seems automatically urged to perform?*

In the T step of the STOP Tool, *the Shema*:

- completing the *heart* part concerns *emotions and memories*;
- the *soul* part includes *judgments* and *forgiveness*;
- the *mind* part involves replacing *lies* with *truth*;
- the *strength* part means listening to the *physical symptoms* in our bodies.

When we have completed the S and T steps, we are ready to "offer the right sacrifice" (O). Ask: *Holy Spirit, what is the right thing to do in this situation now?* Then (P) "put your trust in him" for every outcome.

Take your time and wait on the Holy Spirit through each step, remembering that the STOP Tool will get easier to practice, and then become automatic, because you'll have a wealth of opportunities to practice in plenty more pop quizzes.

V | Verbalize (Pray through your thoughts and emotions.)

Repeat back to him everything you believe he said or revealed. You may want to write your reflections in a journal.[28]

Lord, this STOP Tool made me realize . . .
I had difficulty with . . .
I am afraid of . . .
I need help with . . .

E | Entrust (May it be done to me according to your Word.)

In your Name, Lord Jesus, Son of the living God, I ask you to heal every emotion and judgment associated with this memory, and heal this wound in my soul. Jesus, I ask you to help me to forgive myself and my wounder(s) completely. I renounce the worthlessness lie. I confess my anger and bitterness. I ask you to heal the physical symptoms in my body associated with this pop quiz (name them). I receive and rest in your healing love. Amen.

Six

The Sum of Your Loves

Tools for Continued Whollyness

> My soul magnifies the Lord,
> and my spirit rejoices in God my Savior,
> for he has regarded the low estate of his
>   handmaiden. . . .
> He who is mighty has done great things for me,
> and holy is his name. (Lk 1:46–49)

St. John of the Cross said that in the evening of life, we will be examined in love. Healing, therefore, is a journey of love—heart, soul, mind, and strength—the sum of our loves, we could say. The *Love Heals* book and masterclass give you tools to experience God's love in your deepest wounds.

But many people feel they have never experienced God's love. If this is you, you may feel you're doing something wrong or that God's Word is not true for you. But the scriptures are very clear that God does not lie nor can he lie. It is the enemy who is the liar and the father of lies.

Jeremiah 29:13 assures that "you will seek and find me; when you seek me with your whole heart." The definition of impurity in scripture is to seek God while holding something back, to be double-minded (Jas 1:6–8). The pure in heart "see" God (Mt 5:8). St. Teresa of Ávila agrees: "God withholds himself from no one who perseveres" (*Life*, 10.6). This book has given you some tools of love to facilitate your drawing nearer to God, but we must always remember God is a person who exists in a Trinitarian relationship. We must approach him as a person seeking a relationship, speak to him honestly, open our hearts to him with vulnerability and with truth, and allow him to be honest with us about who we are as well, because often we don't even know ourselves. How do we develop such a relationship with an invisible God? Only love heals, and there is no way to heal fully without an intimate relationship with the Healer, Jesus Christ, in which he pours his love into you and your suffering through his Word.

In all of history, there has never been another book like the scriptures. "The word of God is living and active" (Heb 4:12), so you don't read the Bible like any other book. God, absolute being, makes himself available in its pages for your consideration. You savor it carefully, knowing he's present. You approach the intelligence that imagined and spoke the cosmos into being, expecting to hear his voice. You wait for the sure moment of penetrating truth. You're filled with anticipation of what God will say and do next.

In the Bible, you will discover a heavenly Father who pursues you all your life with holy feet, grips you with the gentlest hands, searches you with sacred eyes, and flies you to heaven in cloudy visions of his face.

Every single day God waits to speak to you with love through the daily Mass readings. The best way to begin healing is to hear God speak, experience his presence, and discern his purpose for your life through the daily readings of the Church. How? LOVE, of course.

Modeled on the annunciation, the LOVE the Word® method invites Our Lady to guide each of us in her own personal prayer practice: L—listen, O—observe, V—verbalize, E—entrust. We learn how to LOVE the Word® like Mary. She teaches us to interpret the Words we hear and read through the landscape of our lives.

Learning to LOVE the Word

How should we begin to read the scriptures this way? Mary models how through the Joyful Mysteries of the Rosary. Her example is an invitation to LOVE the Word with her. I like to practice and teach the steps of lectio divina through what I call the LOVE the Word® Bible reading method:

L | Listen

The Word that I hear and read today is a gift from God in answer to my prayers. So I read the passage slowly. I savor each word as I read, possibly emphasizing each word in turn.

O | Observe

Remembering that I am in the presence of the Holy Spirit, I observe the events of my life with him. Where does this passage speak to the circumstances, relationships, habits, concerns, and problems of the past day? To what word, phrase, or idea is my attention drawn? How is the Holy Spirit guiding and encouraging me today through this passage?

V | Verbalize

As I linger with the Holy Spirit over all that has surfaced in my heart and mind through his Word, I verbalize what I think he is saying to me. I talk to him freely about my thoughts and feelings. I write it all down as best as I understand it and ask him to confirm or deny what I believe he is saying. I will watch to see how he answers by surveying the events of this day and week.

E | Entrust

Once I have decided on some action with his help and in his presence, I am often overwhelmed by the tenderness, patience, mercy, forgiveness, and generosity of God. I resist words now.

As I remain silent and simply rest in him, I entrust him with every outcome.

Mary LOVEs the Word of God so that it comes alive within her and is born into the world. Let us look more closely at her example.

Incarnating the Word of God in the World with Mary

L | Listen

First, Mary listens to the Word of God. In his address in St. Peter's Square, Pope Francis asks,

> What gave rise to Mary's act of going to visit her relative Elizabeth? A word of God's angel. "Elizabeth in her old age has also conceived a son . . ." (Lk 1:36).
>
> Mary knew how to listen to God. But take note: it was not merely "hearing" a superficial word; it was "listening," which consists of attention, acceptance, and availability to God.
>
> It was not in the distracted way with which we sometimes face the Lord or others: we hear their words, but we do not really listen. Mary is attentive to God. She *listens* to God.[1]

Bl. Catherine Emmerich says that when Mary receives the Word of God at the annunciation, she is alone in silence, praying for the promised Messiah. Mary is attentive and available, and she accepts God's answer to her prayers through her "yes" of cooperation: she receives the person of his Word.

Is "listening" simply reading the scriptures? If I read passage after passage, book after book of the Bible, have I really prayed if I have not discerned God as a person there, and adjusted my life to what I have heard? Mary goes further than simply hearing or reading the Word in a cerebral way that does not penetrate or move her. She gives it life by obeying its meaning.

O | Observe

Pope Francis continues,

> "Mary also listens to the events, that is, she interprets the events of her life, she is attentive to reality itself and does not stop on the surface but goes to the depths to grasp its meaning. Her kinswoman Elizabeth, who is already elderly, is expecting a child: this is the event. But Mary is attentive to the meaning. She can understand it: 'with God nothing will be impossible' (Lk 1:37).
>
> "This is also true in our life: listening to God who speaks to us, and listening also to daily reality, paying attention to people, to events, because the Lord is at the door of our life and knocks in many ways, he puts signs on our path; he gives us the ability to see them. Mary is the mother of listening, of attentive listening to God and of equally *attentive listening to the events of life*" (emphasis added).[2]

Mary listens every day in deliberate silence—the "language" of God. She observes the circumstances and relationships in her life through the Word of God she hears. She ponders its meaning in his presence, and rises to obey it. Mary's simple, daily routine is ripe with attention, teeming with potential and significance.

Perhaps Mary taught Jesus this practice, since he followed the same template for listening to God by observing the events and circumstances of his life. He sought secluded spaces to consider how and where and in whom the Father was working, and he joined the Father there:

"Truly, truly, I say to you, the Son can do nothing of his own accord, but only what he sees the Father doing; for whatever he does, that the Son does likewise. For the Father loves the Son, and shows him all that he himself is doing" (Jn 5:19–20).

As St. Gregory says, we "learn the heart of God from the Word of God." Am I available to God's Word every morning? Or am I distracted through activity, noise, and lack of discipline? Do

I read it and hear it with a heart that searches for his perspective in my relationships and circumstances, or am I just completing a religious duty?

Mary "kept all these things, pondering them in her heart" (Lk 2:19). To ponder means "to bring together." Mary gathered the signs and events, all the things God was doing around her. She put them together and meditated on them, seeking connection and meaning. What the angel said, what she heard from Zachariah and Elizabeth, what the shepherds related, she collected in her mind. And drawing the events together, she perceived the meaning of the sweeping truths of her mission and role. Truly, he was God who was born from her.

Where are the connections between the Word I hear today and my current circumstances, relationships, habits, and desires? How does this wisdom fit into long-term events? Do I obey that Word when I receive its perspective on my life?

How do I gather the Word I receive throughout the days and weeks for pondering? I verbalize.

V| Verbalize

When Mary our "mother of listening" receives a whisper of a Word from God in her morning prayer, she hugs the secret close. Going over and over the reality in her mind, she unwraps it carefully with an unspeakable thrill. Looking at its significance from every possible angle, replaying the angel's words, jumping up and down and twirling around in her soul until she's dizzy with the implications. She "ponders it in her heart."

And it is incarnated.

That this unspeakable thing has happened draws a stream of praise, and poetry, and celebration out of her, spreading out in a pool of song that runs up the sides of the hills of history like a wave.

On her way to obey what she has heard and interpreted, Mary prays back to God her understanding of his Word. Her excitement, her awe, her humility, her bliss at being included in such a glorious way in his sweeping, saving plan for all of history is preserved forever in the Church's scripture and liturgy.

"He who sings prays twice," St. Augustine said. The Word of God that Mary has listened to and observed erupts from her in the Magnificat. This is Mary's song. And her song is now the song of the whole Church.

E | Entrust

As Mary entrusts her heart to God in love, he entrusts his Word to her, and she gives birth to that Word in the world, entrusting him to me and you.

At the wedding in Cana, too, Mary brings the Word of God to bear on the practical events and problems of her day and evening. She observes the difficulty of a young married couple at whose wedding feast the wine runs out; she thinks about it.

She knows the Word intimately; to him she verbalizes the problem and entrusts it fully to him: "They have no wine" (Jn 2:3). Mary listens. She observes. She verbalizes. She entrusts. And a miracle occurs.

Experience Your Own Magnificat as You LOVE the Word®

Where is God at work in the relationships and circumstances in our lives? C. S. Lewis said, "Pain is God's megaphone to rouse a deaf world."[3] Where is my pain? Could he be at work there? How will I know if I am not learning to LOVE the Word myself?

In what matter or relationship does he want my cooperation? What do the daily readings say about that today? How do we read and love the Word so that it transforms us and changes the world? We imitate Mary.

Listen, Observe, Verbalize, and *Entrust.* As we go to him in the scriptures on a daily basis, we can use this helpful acronym to discern his activity and will and listen, there, to his voice. We observe our relationships and circumstances and how they connect to the Word we receive each day in the Mass readings.

We verbalize back to God our thoughts and fears and feelings about all of it, what response we think he desires, what we believe he wants us to do. And we fully entrust all that concerns us and our circumstances to him.

"The word of God is living and powerful" (Heb 4:12). When we LOVE the scriptures the way Mary, "mother of listening," teaches us, they come alive in our reality. We bring the power of God's Word to bear on our relationships and circumstances, and as it begins to root and thrive in us, we experience Mary's "Magnificat"—and become a magnificat with her—through the shared thrill of offering the living Word to the world.

Interventions for a Quiet State[4]

Body-based methods and listening to our bodies help us stay in the present moment, the NOW, where healing occurs in Christ. This is the essence of embodiment, or incarnation. Here are some techniques to bring your body back to calmness and relaxation during and after a pop quiz or when feeling anxious.

- Worry box—Only allow yourself fifteen minutes a day on worry. When anxieties pop up and it's not "worry time," put them in a mental box (or write them down and put them in a real box) for later. Then at the scheduled worry time, take them all out and worry over them for fifteen minutes.
- Visualization—Visualize, then distract yourself with "whatever is good, true, lovely, noble . . ." I visualize handing Mary my thoughts, worries, anger, concerns at the foot of the Cross, then get busy doing something else. When the thoughts return, and every time they do, I repeat the visualization, asking her to remove the anger and negativity and help me replace it with thanksgiving. Usually takes a couple of times, and then the negativity and oppression are gone.
- Take a "scan walk"—This is easy when you already enjoy walking, but add a landscape scan, back and forth across the landscape, as you walk for forty-five minutes. It mimics

EMDR and helps the brain process anxiety. Forty-five minutes is the "sweet spot" for processing.
- Create something—Using the right side of the brain helps disengage the left's judgment.
- Block breathing or deep breathing—As I breathe, I like to visualize God's love flowing like a faucet down over my head, all over me, in me, through me, with me.
- TRE exercises—Search "TRE exercise." It's a little disconcerting the first couple of times, but it works! https://traumaprevention.com. I have found it's easiest after exercise, so that your legs are a little wobbly already, then lie down with knees up and open just a little, and let the trembling begin. I do it about fifteen minutes at a time. When they stop trembling at one level of open knees, open them a little more, and again, and then close them a little at a time too. This mimics the trembling that animals do after fight or flight. Ever notice that animals do not experience trauma, even after being stalked and almost eaten by a predator? This is partly why.
- Healing hands—Place a hand on your heart, rub in circles, and send love.
- Music—Like art, music engages the right side of the brain; music, art, prayer all happen in the right side of the brain.
- Gratitude—It's a spiritual principle: negativity multiplies negativity, but thanksgiving multiplies goodness. We see this positive principle at work in Jesus's multiplication of the loaves and fishes.

The following are synopses of further long-term helps included in the Love Heals Masterclass workbook. The stages of faith are from James Fowler's book of the same name;[5] the stages of prayer are from St. John of the Cross's teachings.[6] See the Love Heals Masterclass at sonjacorbitt.com for more on this and all the content in the book.

The next two pages illustrate important stages of spiritual growth, to help you as you continue to discern where God is speaking to you and working in your life.

STAGES OF Faith

 Stage 1 — FORM ATTACHMENTS TO PRIMARY CAREGIVERS. VERBAL, SYMBOLS, AND FAIRY TALES.

 Stage 2 — LEARN WHAT IS REAL AND WHAT IS NOT. BY AGE 10, THINKING IN A LINEAR WAY. LEARNING SYMBOLS OF FAITH.

 Stage 3 — ADOLESCENCE. LEARNING WHO YOU ARE. FAITH BECOMES YOUR OWN.

 Stage 4 — AGES 30-40 YEARS. NOW CONFRONTED WITH BELIEFS THAT ARE DIFFERENT FROM OUR OWN. APPLYING LOGIC TO FAITH.

 Stage 5 — JOINING WHAT WE KNOW AND WHAT WE'VE LEARNED. GROWING IN WISDOM.

 Stage 6 — UNIVERSALIZING FAITH. WE ARE CALLED TO SPEND OURSELVES FOR FAITH.

STAGES OF Prayer

St. John of the Cross

WE BEGIN
THE SPIRITAUL LIFE
WHEN WE BEGIN TO
EARNESTLY SEEK GOD
WITH OUR WHOLE HEART.

purgative

GOD MEETS, WE EXPERIENCE HIS SWEET LOVE.
GOD WITHDRAWS A BIT TO GROW US.
WE CONTINUE THE DISCIPLINE OF PRAYER
WITHOUT THE FEELINGS OF SWEETNESS.
WE LEARN TO LOVE GOD FOR WHO HE IS,
NOT WHAT HE DOES FOR US.

illuminative

PRAYER IS NOW EASY TO PRACTICE.
WE CONSTANTLY REFER BACK TO HIM IN OUR THOUGHTS.
GOD WITHDRAWS AGAIN, SUFFERING MAY COME.
GOD IS PRESENT IN THE SUFFERING.
LEAN INTO THE DARKNESS AND PAIN AND YOU
WILL EXPERIENCE PASSIVE PURIFICATION.

unitive

OUR WILL IS ONE WITH GOD'S.
THE PRAYER IS PURE, THE
PRACTICE OF VIRTUE AND HOLINESS
IS PURE. IT'S ABOUT REST.

Notes

Introduction

1. Benedict XVI, *Jesus of Nazareth* (New York: Doubleday, 2007), 175.
2. Jonathan Fleischmann, "Who Are You, O Immaculate Conception?" Saint Maximilian Kolbe, accessed August 31, 2024, https://saintmaximiliankolbe.com/who-are-you-o-immaculate-conception.
3. See *Litanies of the Heart: Relieving Post-Traumatic Stress and Calming Anxiety through Healing Our Parts* by Gerry Crete (Manchester, NH: Sophia Institute Press, 2023).
4. See Ecclesiastes 11:3, "In the place where the tree falls, there shall it lie." According to the entry for Ecclesiastes 11:3 in the *Haydock Catholic Bible Commentary* (New York: Edward Dunigan and Brother, 1859), e-Sword version, the church fathers understood this verse to mean the following things:

"The state of the soul is unchangeable, when once she comes to heaven or hell: and the soul that departs this life in the state of grace, shall never fall from grace; as on the other side, a soul that dies out of the state of grace, shall never come to it. But this does not exclude a place of temporal punishment for such souls as die in the state of grace: yet not so as to be entirely pure; and therefore they shall be saved, indeed, yet so as by fire, 1 Corinthians iii. 13–15" (Challoner).

"After death, none can merit" (Worthington).

"He who shall not have cultivated his field, (the soul) shall after this life experience the fire of purgation, or eternal punishment" (St. Augustine, *de Gen. contra Man.*, iii. 20).

5. "People are full of internal contradictions: There are many active unconsciousnesses . . . these unconscious processes are living things." Jordan Peterson, personal communication, August 31, 2024, citing the video lecture "Personality: Freud and the Dynamic Unconscious" on the Daily Wire+ app.
6. *The Collected Works of St. John of the Cross*, trans. Kieran Kavanaugh and Otilio Rodriguez (Washington, DC: ICS Publications, 1991), 90.
7. Brennan Mullaney, *Authentic Love: Theory and Therapy* (New York: Society of St. Paul, 2008), 30.
8. Mullaney, *Authentic Love*, 30.

1. Healing Is Sacred

1. I share this account with permission.
2. John Chrysostom, *Three Homilies on the Devil*, trans. Bryson Sewell, 2014, homily 2, sec. V, https://archive.org/details/chrysostom-devil-bryson-2014.

3. Francis, "Recital of the Holy Rosary for the Conclusion of the Marian Month of May," vatican.va, accessed September 2, 2024, https://www.vatican.va/content/francesco/en/speeches/2013/may/documents/papa-francesco_20130531_conclusione-mese-mariano.html.

4. See chapter 5 on purgatory, "Perfected by His Presence," in *Fulfilled: Uncovering the Biblical Foundations of Catholicism*, by Sonja Corbitt (West Chester, PA: Ascension Press, 2018), 107–125.

5. Arthur Janov, *The Biology of Love* (Amherst, NY: Prometheus Books, 2000), 272.

6. Mullaney, *Authentic Love*, xix. See also 1 John 4:18.

7. Benedict XVI, *Jesus of Nazareth*, 177.

2. With All Your Heart

1. See also John 9:2.

2. "People are full of internal contradictions: There are many active unconsciousnesses . . . these unconscious processes are living things." Jordan Peterson, personal communication, August 31, 2024, citing the video lecture "Personality: Freud and the Dynamic Unconscious" on the Daily Wire+ app.

3. M. Scott Peck, *The Road Less Traveled* (New York: Touchstone, 2003), 15–18.

4. Plants have an *animative* soul that provides the general necessities of life; animals have a *sensitive* soul that can respond to input from the senses; both are non-spiritual and therefore finite; the souls of plants and animals cease to exist at death. Humans, on the other hand, have a *rational* spiritual soul that knows and understands good and evil and makes decisions from such knowledge. Angels are pure, rational spirits without bodies. Humans are unique in creation as creatures of both rational soul (spirit) and body. See Thomas Aquinas, *The Summa Theologiae of St. Thomas Aquinas*, 2nd ed., trans. Fathers of the English Dominican Province, prima pars, q. 78, https://www.newadvent.org/summa/1078.htm.

5. A convenient STOP Tool printable with all the steps is available at becauseloveheals.com.

6. Aquinas, *The Summa Theologiae of St. Thomas Aquinas*, secunda secundae partis, q. 158, https://www.newadvent.org/summa/3158.htm.

7. Adapted from Encounter School of Ministry's "Ministering to Wounded Memories" worksheet and the John Paul II Healing Center's "In-Depth Ministry Prayer."

8. Peck, *The Road Less Traveled*, 81.

9. See Matthew 18, the Love Heals Masterclass, and the Love Heals podcast series on sonjacorbitt.com.

10. Guidance in "complete" forgiveness according to Matthew 18 principles takes about an hour, and it is best facilitated and most effective with an experienced spiritual director in a deliverance exercise that targets the lie and opposite virtue in each offense the Holy Spirit brings to memory. But you can begin by simply asking the Holy Spirit to bring to mind any and all offenses that you need to forgive. Start with your mom and dad, move to yourself, God, your spouse, and anyone or anything else. Although God does not do things that need our forgiveness, we sometimes hold

resentments toward him for things he allows, so ask him. Perhaps you bring them all to the foot of the Cross and leave them there. When the Holy Spirit brings nothing else to mind, thank him and walk in love.

11. This is called the "Principle of First Use."
12. Julian of Norwich, *Revelation of Love* (New York: Doubleday, 1996), 91.
13. I share this with their permission.
14. See also *The Little Way: Healing the Inner Child* podcast series on sonjacorbitt.com.
15. LOVE the Word® Mary journals for this purpose are available at sonjacorbitt.com.

3. With All Your Soul

1. See 2 Kings 17:29–33. After the kingdom split, General Jeroboam took the ten Northern tribes (later the Samaritans) and established apostate worship in various historically significant locations to prevent the people from traveling to the glorious Temple in Jerusalem for the Jewish feasts. Later, these tribes were conquered by Assyrians who established five deities, collectively called Baals.
2. The Pontifical Council for Culture and the Pontifical Council for Interreligious Dialogue, *Jesus Christ, the Bearer of the Water of Life: A Christian Reflection on the "New Age,"* vatican.va, accessed September 3, 2024, https://www.vatican.va/roman_curia/pontifical_councils/interelg/documents/rc_pc_interelg_doc_20030203_new-age_en.html.
3. Clement of Alexandria, *Church Fathers: The Paedagogus*, trans. William Wilson, from *Ante-Nicene Fathers*, vol. 2, ed. Alexander Roberts, James Donaldson, and A. Cleveland Coxe (Buffalo, NY: Christian Literature Publishing, 1885), revised and edited for New Advent by Kevin Knight, https://www.newadvent.org/fathers/02093.htm.
4. Fernand Cabrol, "Christian Worship," *The Catholic Encyclopedia*, vol. 15 (New York: Robert Appleton Company, 1912), http://www.newadvent.org/cathen/15710a.htm.
5. Lisa Miller, *The Awakened Brain: The Psychology of Spirituality* (London: Penguin 2021), 58, 153–154.
6. See *Fulfilled: Uncovering the Biblical Foundations of Catholicism*, by Sonja Corbitt (West Chester, PA: Ascension Press, 2018).
7. Augustine of Hippo, *On the Catechizing of the Uninstructed*, trans. S. D. F. Salmond, from *Nicene and Post-Nicene Fathers*, first series, vol. 3, ed. Philip Schaff (Buffalo, NY: Christian Literature Publishing, 1887), revised and edited for New Advent by Kevin Knight, https://www.newadvent.org/fathers/1303.htm.
8. Lembas or waybread in J. R. R. Tolkien's *The Lord of the Rings*.
9. For an overview on attachment styles and insecure attachment in particular, see "Attachment Styles," Cleveland Clinic, last updated August 4, 2023, https://my.clevelandclinic.org/health/articles/25170-attachment-styles. For more academic and in-depth articles, search https://scholar.google.com with keywords: anxiety+insecure+mother+attachments.
10. Helen F. Bergin, "Living One's Truth," *The Furrow* 51, no. 1 (2000): 15.

11. See chapter 3, endnote 1 on the Jew-Samaritan split.

12. Augustine of Hippo, *Exposition on Psalm 51*, trans. J. E. Tweed, from *Nicene and Post-Nicene Fathers*, first series, vol. 8, edited by Philip Schaff (Buffalo, NY: Christian Literature Publishing Co., 1888), revised and edited for New Advent by Kevin Knight, https://www.newadvent.org/fathers/1801051.htm.

13. *The Collected Works of St. John of the Cross*, 90.

14. Jordan Peterson, personal communication, August 31, 2024, citing the video lecture "Adam and Eve: Self-Consciousness, Evil, and Death" on the Daily Wire+ app.

15. C. G. Jung, *Aion: Researches into the Phenomenology of the Self* (Princeton, NJ: Princeton University Press, 1969), 9.

16. C. G. Jung, *Archetypes of the Unconscious* (Princeton, NJ: Princeton University Press, 1969), 317.

17. Chad Ripperger, *Dominion: The Nature of Diabolic Warfare* (Keenesburg, CO: Sensus Traditionis Press, 2021), 205.

18. Guidance in "complete" forgiveness according to Matthew 18 principles takes about an hour, and it is best facilitated and most effective with an experienced spiritual director in a deliverance exercise that targets the lie and opposite virtue in each offense the Holy Spirit brings to memory. But you can begin by simply asking the Holy Spirit to bring to mind any and all offenses that you need to forgive. Start with your mom and dad, and then move to yourself, God, your spouse, and anyone or anything else. Although God does not do things that need our forgiveness, we sometimes hold resentments toward him for things he allows; so ask him. Perhaps you bring them all to the foot of the Cross and leave them there. When the Holy Spirit brings nothing else to mind, thank him and walk in love.

19. The Pontifical Council for Culture and the Pontifical Council for Interreligious Dialogue, *Jesus Christ, the Bearer of the Water of Life: A Christian Reflection on the "New Age,"* Vatican.va, accessed September 3, 2024, sec. 5, https://www.vatican.va/roman_curia/pontifical_councils/interelg/documents/rc_pc_interelg_doc_20030203_new-age_en.html.

20. See Jordan Peterson's big five personality test, "Understand Myself," at Understandmyself.com, 2024, https://www.understandmyself.com.

21. If you begin to panic, stop and seek professional help.

22. LOVE the Word® Mary journals for this purpose are available at sonjacorbitt.com.

4. With All Your Mind

1. See Sonja Corbitt, *Just Rest: Receiving God's Renewing Presence in the Deserts of Your Life* (Notre Dame, IN: Ave Maria Press, 2021).

2. Corbitt, *Just Rest*.

3. "Cockroach," Wikipedia, accessed April 29, 2024, https://en.wikipedia.org/wiki/cockroach.

4. Caroline Leaf, *Who Switched Off My Brain?* (Southlake, TX: Thomas Nelson, 2009), 22.

5. Aquinas, *Summa Theologiae*, prima secundae partis, q. 22, https://www.newadvent.org/summa/2022.htm.
6. Daniel Goleman, *Emotional Intelligence: Why It Can Matter More Than IQ* (New York: Bantam, 1995).
7. For more information, visit sonjacorbitt.com.
8. Julian of Norwich, *Revelation of Love* (New York: Doubleday, 1996), 91–92.
9. If you begin to panic, stop, and seek professional help.
10. Adapted from Encounter School of Ministry's *Ministering to Wounded Memories* and JPII Healing Center's *In-Depth Ministry Prayer*.
11. LOVE the Word® Mary journals for this purpose are available at sonjacorbitt.com.

5. With All Your Strength

1. The Hebrew word for "mother."
2. Bessel Van Der Kolk, *The Body Keeps the Score: Brain, Mind, and Body in the Healing of Trauma* (New York: Penguin Books, 2014).
3. See Exodus 15:26, 2 Kings 5:1–14, Isaiah 38:21, Jeremiah 30:17, and Psalm 103:2–3, among many others.
4. *Orthodox Psychotherapy: The Science of the Fathers*, trans. Esther Williams (Levadia, Greece: Birth of the Theotokos Monastery, 2020), 122–126.
5. Benedict XVI, *Jesus of Nazareth*, 175.
6. Kassem Sharif et al., "The Role of Stress in the Mosaic of Autoimmunity: An Overlooked Association," *Autoimmunity Reviews* 17, no. 10 (2018), https://doi.org/10.1016/j.autrev.2018.04.005; Aditi Nerurkar et al., "When Physicians Counsel About Stress: Results of a National Study," *JAMA Internal Medicine* 173, no. 1 (2013), https://jamanetwork.com/journals/jamainternalmedicine/fullarticle/1392494.
7. Congregation for the Doctrine of the Faith, "Instruction on Prayers for Healing," vatican.va, accessed September 4, 2024, https://www.vatican.va/roman_curia/congregations/cfaith/documents/rc_con_cfaith_doc_20001123_istruzione_en.html.
8. This trembling and shaking is mimicked for humans in a therapy called Tension and Trauma Releasing Exercises, or TRE.
9. Peter Levine, *Waking the Tiger: The Innate Capacity to Transform Overwhelming Experiences* (Berkeley, CA: North Atlantic Books, 1997), 85–86.
10. Thomas Aquinas, *Summa Theologiae*, prima secundae partis, q. 22. https://www.newadvent.org/summa/2022.htm.
11. Levine, *Waking the Tiger*, 85–86.
12. For more on the link between suppressed anger and breast cancer, see S. Greer and Tina Morris, "Psychological Attributes of Women Who Develop Breast Cancer: A Controlled Study," *Journal of Psychosomatic Research* 19, no. 2 (1975), https://www.sciencedirect.com/science/article/abs/pii/0022399975900628.

On the link between emotional suppression and all-cause mortality, see Benjamin P. Chapman et al., "Emotion Suppression and Mortality Risk over a 12-Year Follow-Up," *Journal of Psychosomatic Research* 75, no. 4 (2013), https://www.ncbi.nlm.nih.gov/pmc/articles/PMC3939772, and Ernest Harburg et al., "Expressive/

Suppressive Anger-Coping Responses, Gender, and Types of Mortality: A 17-Year Follow-Up (Tecumseh, Michigan, 1971–1988)," *Psychosomatic Medicine* 65, no. 4 (2003), http://www.ncbi.nlm.nih.gov/pubmed/12883109.

On the link between suppressed anger and prostate cancer, see Frank J. Penedo et al., "Anger Suppression Mediates the Relationship between Optimism and Natural Killer Cell Cytotoxicity in Men Treated for Localized Prostate Cancer," *Journal of Psychosomatic Research* 60, no. 4 (2006), http://www.ncbi.nlm.nih.gov/pubmed/16581368.

On the link between suppressed emotion and back pain, see John Sarno, *Healing Back Pain: The Mind-Body Connection* (New York: Hachette Book Group, 1991).

13. See https://www.sonjacorbitt.com/masterclass-2/ for details.

14. Sometimes it describes the worshipping cherubim on the Ark whose wings "covered" the mercy seat.

15. Billy Swan, "Unpacking One of Newman's Gems," Word on Fire, November 15, 2019, https://www.wordonfire.org/articles/unpacking-one-of-newmans-gems.

16. There are others, included in the Love Heals Masterclass, but for the sake of brevity, I only include two.

17. Search https://scholar.google.com with search words: attachment+theory.

18. See Carl Jung, "The Syzygy," in *Aion: Researches into the Phenomenology of the Self*, and "Conscious, Unconscious, and Individuation," in *The Archetypes and the Collective Unconscious*.

19. Blaise Pascal, *Pensées* (New York: Penguin Books, 1966), 75.

20. Mark A. Lumley et al., "Emotional Awareness and Expression Therapy, Cognitive Behavioral Therapy, and Education for Fibromyalgia: A Cluster-Randomized Controlled Trial," *Pain* 158, no. 12 (2017), https://pubmed.ncbi.nlm.nih.gov/28796118.

21. "Psycho-oncology: Discover How Stress Causes Cancer," Puna Wai Ora Mind-Body Cancer Clinic, accessed September 4, 2024, https://www.alternative-cancer-care.com, and "The Link between Cancer and Unexpressed Anger," Puna Wai Ora Mind-Body Cancer Clinic, accessed September 4, 2024, https://www.alternative-cancer-care.com/cancer-anger-link.html.

22. Amanda J. Burger et al., "The Effects of a Novel Psychological Attribution and Emotional Awareness and Expression Therapy for Chronic Musculoskeletal Pain: A Preliminary, Uncontrolled Trial," *Journal of Psychosomatic Research* 81, no. 1 (2016), https://pubmed.ncbi.nlm.nih.gov/26800632.

23. Levine, *Waking the Tiger*, 17, 83, 133–134.

24. See www.sonjacorbitt.com/category/somata.

25. Interestingly, this is the sign in American Sign Language for "I'm sorry."

26. Levine, *Waking the Tiger*, 79.

27. If you begin to panic, stop and seek professional help.

28. LOVE the Word® Mary journals for this purpose are available at sonjacorbitt.com.

6. The Sum of Your Loves

1. Francis, "Recital of the Holy Rosary for the Conclusion of the Marian Month of May," 1.

2. Francis, "Recital of the Holy Rosary for the Conclusion of the Marian Month of May," 1.
3. C. S. Lewis, *The Problem of Pain* (San Francisco, CA: HarperOne, 2003), 93.
4. See the Love Heals Masterclass at sonjacorbitt.com for more on this and all the content in the book.
5. James W. Fowler, *Stages of Faith* (New York: HarperCollins, 1995).
6. *The Collected Works of St. John of the Cross.*

Sonja Corbitt is a Catholic author and speaker who has produced several multimedia Bible studies, including *Unleashed, Fearless, Exalted,* and *Just Rest.* She also created the LOVE the Word® Bible study method.

Corbitt is host of the *Sacred Healing 12:30* podcast and the *Evangelista Bible Study* show on CatholicTV. She has decades of experience and training from Holy Apostles College and Seminary, the Catholic Psychotherapy Association, the John Paul II Healing Center, the Encounter School of Ministry, and Unbound.

A Carolina native who was raised as a Southern Baptist, Corbitt attended Mitchell College and the Southern Baptist Theological Seminary center in Jackson, Tennessee, before converting to Catholicism. She has since served as director of religious education at St. John Vianney Catholic Church in Gallatin, Tennessee, and executive director of Risen Radio in Lebanon, Tennessee.

She lives in Tennessee with her husband, Bob, and their two sons.

sonjacorbitt.com
Facebook: @sonjacorbitt
Instagram: @sonjacorbittevangelista
Pinterest: @sonjacorbitt

MORE FROM
SONJA CORBITT

Unleashed
How to Receive Everything the Holy Spirit Wants to Give You

In *Unleashed*, Sonja Corbitt shares her passion for the scriptures by weaving the Word of God with her own experiences to show readers how the Holy Spirit flows through their lives in relationships, prayer, and times of suffering.

Just Rest
Receiving God's Renewing Presence in the Desert

Just Rest, a five-week Bible study on the Exodus account, will help you to apply its spiritual lessons in your own life, identify areas of desolation and need, and better understand God's greater purposes in times of adversity and dryness.
In so doing, you will experience what it means to invite Jesus to nourish your spirit and guide you to the kingdom promised to all who enter into his rest.

Fearless
Conquer Your Demons and Love with Abandon

What are the sources of anxiety, stress, and fear you experience in your life? Sonja Corbitt believes that these often-paralyzing emotions are the direct result of our everyday battles against sin and temptation. In *Fearless*, she equips us with the spiritual tools we need to restore our spiritual well-being.

Exalted
How the Power of the Magnificat Can Transform Us

Combining her own story with an invitation to engage the scriptures through personal study and "God prompts," Sonja Corbitt will help you to unlock the treasures contained within Mary's *Magnificat*, revealing a song that speaks to each of us in a unique way, calling us to delight in the power of God to transform us and make us into everything he created us to be so we can revel in the fullness and joy of life in Christ.

Look for these titles wherever books and eBooks are sold.
Visit **avemariapress.com** for more information.